Prosperity with Principles

Prosperity with Principles:
Some Policies for Economic Growth

David G. Green

Civitas: Institute for the Study of Civil Society
London

First Published April 2010

© Civitas 2010
55 Tufton Street
London SW1P 3QL
Civitas is a registered charity (no. 1085494)
and a company limited by guarantee, registered in
England and Wales (no. 04023541)

email: books@civitas.org.uk

ISBN 978-1-906837-13-6

Independence: Civitas: Institute for the Study of Civil
Society is a registered educational charity (No. 1085494) and
a company limited by guarantee (No. 04023541). Civitas is
financed from a variety of private sources to avoid over-
reliance on any single or small group of donors.

All publications are independently refereed. All the Institute's
publications seek to further its objective of promoting the
advancement of learning. The views expressed are those of
the authors, not of the Institute.

Typeset by
Civitas

Printed in Great Britain by
Cromwell Press Group
Trowbridge, Wiltshire

Contents

Author

David G. Green is the Director of Civitas. His books include *The New Right: The Counter Revolution in Political, Economic and Social Thought*, Wheatsheaf, 1987; *Reinventing Civil Society*, IEA, 1993; *Community Without Politics: A Market Approach to Welfare Reform*, IEA 1996; *Benefit Dependency: How Welfare Undermines Independence*, IEA, 1999; *We're (Nearly) All Victims Now*, Civitas 2006 and *Individualists Who Co-operate*, Civitas 2009. He contributed an essay to *Nations Choose Prosperity* (Ruth Lea, ed.), Civitas 2009.

He writes occasionally for newspapers, including in recent years pieces in *The Times* and *The Sunday Times*, the *Sunday Telegraph* and the *Daily Telegraph*.

Preface

The recession has sparked a debate about the renewal of manufacturing and it is now generally accepted that the government should create the conditions in which manufacturing can flourish. But, how it should do so is strongly disputed.

I am going to advocate 'prosperity policy' to avoid confusion with the 'industrial policy' pursued in the 1960s and 1970s. If the term 'industrial policy' has a distinct meaning it is 'selective industrial policy', and as such it is associated with the discredited anti-competitive policies of national plans and national champions pursued in the 1960s and 1970s. Moreover, to speak of industrial policy implies that manufacturing industry is the main concern and, while a renewal is long overdue and indispensable for any economic revival, it is not the only consideration. The folly of welcoming post-industrial society and denigrating 'metal bashing' is now obvious, but our future prosperity depends on encouraging every kind of productive activity, manufacturing included.

But economic growth at any cost should not be the objective of policy. One of the worst mistakes of the Blair and Brown administrations has been their focus on promoting short-term economic growth regardless of the impact on the social fabric. As Nick Cohen remarked in a recent article in *Standpoint*, free markets were pursued, not reluctantly, but 'joyously and with the fervour of an Ayn Rand cultist'.[1] So-called light-touch regulation of financial markets was a primary cause of the financial crisis. By reducing regulation in the hope of attracting banks to locate in London rather than New York, the Government undermined the efforts of American legislators to curtail the most dubious banking practices.[2] Mass immigration was also encouraged because it was believed to create growth and reduce inflation by driving down wages. The impact on public services and the lives of ordinary people were disregarded. We need economic growth more than ever, but it needs to be tempered by some higher principles.

In particular, if we want to continue being a prosperous and principled people, the quest for growth should be mitigated by a concern for the kind of equality that is compatible with liberty and prosperity for all. This requirement rules out the enforced equalization of income at the hands of state agencies and instead points to public policies that offer a fighting chance for everyone to give of their best. In our efforts to re-establish a more balanced economy, for example, we should aim for a human balance as well as an economic balance—diversity that creates opportunities for our varied talents as well as protecting us from over-reliance on one economic sector.

And in reforming our commercial institutions, including banks and business corporations, we should aim to facilitate a renewal of commercial enterprises whose leaders face economic realities when they have to but who are prepared to put up a fight to maintain a future for their employees. Business leadership should be a vocation, not a relentless search for the best return on capital to the exclusion of all other human responsibilities. Warren Buffett, one of the most successful investors of all time, famously gives three instructions to the chief executive officers of his numerous business. They are to run their business as if (1) they are the sole owner; (2) it is the only asset they hold; and (3) they can never sell or merge it for 100 years. The reform of the trade unions in the 1980s has been vital in opening up new possibilities. The legal privileges given to unions in 1906— which Keynes described as having turned those who were once oppressed into tyrants—encouraged the making of mutually destructive demands.[3] As a result of the moderation of union power, during the last couple of years tens of thousands of jobs have been saved as employers and employees in countless workplaces have agreed to reduce or restrain wages to keep their enterprise alive. This new industrial climate opens the way for a more co-operative future in which the maximisation of shareholder value is seen for the shallow mockery of the ideal of free enterprise that it is.

I will take particular issue with two arguments that are major stumbling blocks to discussion of a pragmatic approach to 'prosperity policy'. The first is doctrinal non-interventionism, a general hostility to government action that still pervades discussion even when it is formally renounced. I will argue that, while adhering to liberal principles, nations should adopt the policies that work for them. There is more than one liberal path to prosperity. The second is a tendency to confuse all patriotism with aggressive nationalism. I will argue that it is perfectly possibly to be legitimately patriotic, to refrain from nationalistic animosity, and yet unashamedly to pursue our national interests in a spirit compatible with international reciprocity. Just as each one of us owes to everyone else in Britain the obligation to earn a living in order to do our bit, so in international relations we should aim to become prosperous enough to be able to engage in mutually beneficial trade and, where necessary, to assist the people of other lands. But to be of any use to other people we need to be wealthy in the first place.

I will suggest some public policies that would encourage manufacturing without compromising our commitment to free enterprise. Success in manufacturing, especially in all-important export markets, depends on having a comparative advantage. Such advantages—including the price, avail-ability and quality—often depend on individual companies, but they also depend on the government. Above all, some such advantages can only be created by the government as part of its inescapable responsibility for creating conditions consistent with productive enterprise, including taxation, regulation, the cost of energy and much more.

I am very grateful to Tim Congdon, Ruth Lea, Lee Craven, Richard Smith, Ivan Bradbury, Carl Griffin, Dominic Hobson, Claire Daley, Catherine Green and David Grove for either reading a draft of this paper or giving up their time to discuss the proposals. It hardly needs to be said that they do not necessarily agree with the final product—far from it in some cases.

David Green

Introduction

Does manufacturing matter? A glance at the top 20 most wealthy countries per head of population suggests that, unless blessed by ample reserves of oil and natural gas, it is impossible for a major nation to prosper without a significant manufacturing sector. The people of a country can support themselves by growing crops, raising animals, fishing, extracting minerals from the ground, adding value to raw materials (manufacturing), or providing services such as transport and banking or insurance. In our case, we do not have the option of supporting 60 million people from our oil and natural gas reserves (as smaller countries in the top 20 like Qatar and Brunei do). We must rely on all the options available to us, including agriculture, fishing, mining, financial and business services, and manufacturing —unless we are willing either to live at a lower material standard or to emigrate in large numbers. During the final quarter of the nineteenth century many who were squeezed out of agriculture, for example, left for overseas, a trend that was particularly strong in Ireland. And today, many people try to leave poorer countries to work in the West.

We can safely say that, if we want to make it possible for the current population to live at the current standard or higher, then we will need a significant manufacturing sector. In addition, there is a question of balance. A nation that puts too much faith in one major export earner is highly vulnerable to external fluctuations. Economic balance is, therefore, wise. But, there is a second balance that a government can legitimately pursue: a human balance. A good society should aim to provide outlets for all human talents and aptitudes.

Some further preliminary remarks are called for. I am convinced that we need to revive manufacturing. Some people accept that we should encourage high-value productive activity but contend that some manufacturing is of low-value and not worth bothering with. However, low-value products are typically part of a supply chain that has a high-value finished product at the end. The physical proximity of manufacturer and sub-contractor may be a vital element in the success of both. In any event, a public policy should not favour or disfavour high-value or low-value activity. Competition can be left to take its course.

More important, when I speak of manufacturing I am not making a contrast with 'services', and certainly not implying that services are inferior. In any event, many of our leading manufacturers also provide services. Rolls-Royce, for example, manufactures aero engines but also services them throughout their working life, and a good deal of its income comes from these service contracts. The aim of public policy should be to provide favourable conditions for productive activity, whether it involves making things or providing services.

One final reason for avoiding a comparison between manufacturing and services is that the way in which manufacturing is measured by the Office for National Statistics is rather misleading, especially when making comparisons over time. For example, 30 years ago a manufacturing industry like shipbuilding would have had huge offices with row upon row of technicians producing technical drawings. Sometimes this work was sub-contracted, in which case it was re-classified as a service in the official statistics. Today such work is not only outsourced but also performed by far fewer people using computer-aided design systems. But even if a design firm works totally for manufacturers its work is officially a service. According to the Government, between 1998 and 2006 'reclassification' accounted for the loss of 120,000 jobs from manufacturing, about 10 per cent of the total fall.[1] In other words, the contribution being made by manufacturing to our economic survival is somewhat greater than it looks at first sight. How far should the government go to revive manufacturing? Are tax subsidies justified? Is protection from imports necessary? Should governments do anything at all, beyond maintaining law and order and a welfare safety net?

Once we start to ask ourselves what the government should do, we run into long-established theories about the merits and demerits of government action. We have a long liberal heritage of mistrusting political power, initially based on its abuse in the days of royal absolutism. Since the seventeenth century two main anti-absolutist traditions evolved: non-interventionism (laissez-faire) and liberal-democracy. It is impossible to discuss government policy towards manufacturing without clarifying what is at stake between the champions of laissez-faire, on the one hand, and liberal democracy on the other.

Further discussion follows in chapter 2, but for now we can say that non-interventionism is the view that policy should aim primarily to get the government out of the way, especially by reducing taxes and de-regulating. Unfortunately the champions of non-intervention have misunderstood the liberal tradition. They are inclined to assume that there is a natural state of affairs that will emerge in the absence of state coercion. Consequently every reduction in regulation is seen as an increase in individual freedom, when it may be no such thing. As I will show, the great liberal thinkers did not see small government as the ultimate aim. Instead they wanted liberal government—a system established to make possible the kind of personal freedom that could be enjoyed by everyone. They sought 'civic freedom' not 'wild freedom' —

in the terminology of one of the greatest Enlightenment philosophers.[2] The chief problem of our political system today is that the government at any one time is dominated by a political party that may abuse its power to reward its followers or to perpetuate itself in office at the expense of democratic rivals. If it seeks future electoral support because it has been a good servant of our common interests there is no objection, but it is very easy for policies that can be justified as mutually beneficial to be twisted into instruments for the retention of power. If industries are to be supported with taxpayers' funds then past experience has provided ample evidence of the dangers, including the wasteful subsidisation of badly-run businesses that happen to be well-connected politically.

Some critics advocate total non-intervention as a solution to such cronyism, but as I have argued, this attitude misunderstands the kind of freedom that is available to the members of a group of people as distinct from an isolated individual. The liberal-democratic approach is to guard against the abuse of power through checks and balances and constitutional safeguards. Cronyism is not of itself a reason for inaction. It is a perennial risk that needs to be guarded against.

Another view, linked to non-interventionism, is that the officials and politicians who make up the government will tend to make worse decisions than investors who take risks with their own money. The latter will tend to take more trouble to appraise projects at the outset and will be quicker to pull out when things go wrong. So, in addition to the risk that taxpayers' money will be used to retain a ruling party in power, government officials may also be reckless in investing other people's cash and slow to detect failure.

4

These are real dangers. However, as a matter of simple observation, many governments in Britain and elsewhere have provided subsidies and 'picked winners' successfully. Some examples are described in chapter 1. A doctrinaire view is not, therefore, justified. We should learn from the known successes and build in safeguards against the known risks.

We should also remind ourselves how business really works. The case for unfettered free trade is based on the pursuit of low production costs—relative to other realistically attainable alternatives—above everything else. But is it how businesses really conduct themselves? In practice, many business models aim to maintain high prices so that their workforce can earn more. For example, they try to invent a product that can be patented, so that they will not face serious price competition for a specified number of years. In some parts of the world, such as northern Italy, the textile and leather industries have stayed put despite the fact that the work is labour intensive and could be carried out for a lower labour cost overseas. They succeed by commanding a higher price because of their design qualities. A bigger share of the profits is taken by the workforce, but such businesses remain profitable. It is not the highest virtue to push wages down to the lowest level currently payable anywhere in the world. A free enterprise society should not be seen as one in which cheapness is put above every other concern. It is rather a state of affairs in which any enterprise capable of self-support is able to flourish. If the owner is willing to share a higher proportion of the profit with the workforce, why should anyone object?

Advocates of free trade assume that lower prices will follow, that competition will increase, and that the short-term losers will move to more productive work. However, as a matter of observation, they sometimes do and sometimes don't. These concerns draw us to the question famously asked by Adam Smith: What are the causes of the wealth of nations? He asked it, not because he believed that the less the government did the better it would be for everyone, but rather because he thought that a free people needed to give constant, detailed attention to the 'rules of the game'. Smith perceived political economy to be 'the science of a statesman or legislator' and identified two main aims of public policy. The first was to provide a plentiful subsistence for the people, or 'more properly to enable them to provide such a revenue or subsistence for themselves'; and the second 'to supply a state or common-wealth with a revenue sufficient for the public services'.[3]

Over the last 200 years support for different ideas about how to achieve these aims has ebbed and flowed. In Britain debate has tended to polarise between theories advocating big and small government. From the end of World War Two until the 1970s there was great faith in the power of government to create a 'plentiful subsistence'. Some indust-ries were nationalised, many that remained private were forcibly consolidated, and the rest were subject to nationally planned objectives. Private investment income was subject to punitive rates of taxation.

By the late 1970s this approach was judged to have failed and was replaced by free-market policies under Thatcher and Major, and largely continued under Blair and Brown, although with a stronger penchant for regulation than under the Tories. Now, however, the financial crisis has been blamed on too much laissez-faire and books are being written about the failure of capitalism—not only by diehard collectivists who always opposed the Thatcherite revival but by authors, such as Richard Posner, who have championed liberal-market philosophy for decades. Roger Bootle's fine book, *The Trouble With Markets*, also identifies some fundamental flaws in the global financial system and the distinguished chief economics commentator of the *Financial Times*, Martin Wolf, has grappled with how best to control the financial manias that have become prevalent following the collapse of the Bretton Woods agreement during the 1970s.[4]

Chapter 1 discusses the experience of developing countries in recent years. Just as Adam Smith tried to understand the realities of his own time, so we should try to make sense of the experience of nations who have grown wealthy in the last half century. Because we are an advanced economy and still one of the most prosperous nations, our policy makers have not paid much attention to the debates among development economists. But their concerns do not apply to less-wealthy countries alone. No country ever stops being a developing economy and there is much that we can learn.

Chapter 2 describes how our heritage of liberalism differs from the formulaic non-interventionism that has distorted our understanding in recent years. It argues that a free society is a free people with a state committed to personal freedom; not a group of people without a state or with only a tiny government. Freedom is a contrivance of politics, not a spontaneous state of affairs. It requires a government strong enough to police a society based on mutual agreement, but not so strong that it becomes an uncontrollable threat to individual liberty. This classical-liberal formula is the highest ideal to which humans have aspired. So far, it has not been achieved in full, although we have made significant strides in the right direction. The struggle continues.

Moreover, we should never forget that the primary aim is to grant everyone the personal freedom to seek out the heights of human achievement, whether in the mundane affairs of daily life or by aiming at the pinnacles of success in art, literature, sport, science, medicine, education, manufacturing, philanthropy, religion or other walks of life. Individual freedom has led to great increases in prosperity, but more wealth is not the principal aim. If freedom could only be secured at a lower standard of living then so be it. Freedom comes first. It is with this qualification in mind that this book advocates 'prosperity policy'.

Chapter 3 turns to public policy recommendations.

1

We Are All Developing Countries Now

What can we learn from the experience of developing countries? As the first country to industrialise and as one of the most prosperous nations in existence, we tend to see ourselves in a different light from developing nations. But the scale of industrial decline combined with the weakness of our public finances has made this attitude a luxury we can't afford. If we do not play our hand well, we could find ourselves declining still further. We should not, therefore, be too proud to learn from nations that have enjoyed rapid growth in recent years.

Throughout the modern era nations have asked how best they can create the material wealth, not merely to feed, clothe and house themselves, but also to improve their civilisation. When Adam Smith looked back through history in the 1770s he concluded that the wealthiest nations had benefited from governments that allowed their people to use their energy and initiative to produce goods and services as they believed best. He also noticed that nations that were reasonably open to trade with their neighbours were more prosperous than those that were not. Specialisation allowed individuals to be more productive and thus able to accumulate capital, which allowed them to further improve their land, crops, animal husbandry, transport and the manufacture of goods. And when the most efficient specialised producers traded with each other, all tended to be better off.

His approach worked for Britain, but America and Germany, especially from the 1860s onwards, used tariffs to keep British products out and to develop their own manufactures. They had overtaken Britain by the early twentieth century thus contradicting Smith's view that only countries most open to trade became the most prosperous. It had proved possible to gain in prosperity as a result of protectionism.

After the Second World War GATT (later the WTO) entrenched a certain amount of free trade but many nations that became more prosperous in the 1960s and 70s used import substitution, state-owned enterprises, foreign-exchange controls, state investment planning and price controls. Nevertheless, by the late 1970s attitudes were reversing and a new confidence in free markets emerged, later called globalisation. From the 1980s the intellectual consensus was in favour of a revitalised free-market doctrine.

Gobind Nankani, now vice-president for the Africa World Bank, has summed up the view that prevailed at the World Bank in the early 1990s. Government interference in the economy 'through price controls, foreign exchange rationing, distorted trade regimes, repressed financial markets, and state ownership of commercial enterprises' was considered to have 'wasted resources and impeded growth'.[1] The policy conclusion was that 'rolling back the state would lead developing countries to sustained growth'. This view came to be called the Washington Consensus following a book by John Williamson in 1990. According to Nankani, it was 'the dominant view, making it difficult for others to be heard' and provided the framework for many of the reforms implemented during the 1990s.[2] Nations that came to the International Monetary Fund (IMF) for loans found that they were pushed into de-regulation, privatisation and the extension of free trade. And, the World Bank used its grants to encourage similar policies.

By the beginning of the twenty-first century, however, this new consensus was being challenged. The results had not been as predicted and a major change of heart is captured in a 2005 World Bank report that appraises the policies pursued by the Bank during the 1990s. By 2005 the World Bank felt that the results of its policies had exceeded hopes in some cases but in others 'fell well short of expectations'.[3] Washington-Consensus policies had failed in Latin America, Russia, and Africa. There had been partial success in the Czech Republic, Hungary and Poland, but Mexico (1994), East Asia (1997), Brazil (1998), the Russian Federation (1998), Turkey (2000) and Argentina (2002) had gone through financial crises. The World Bank confessed to being surprised that Russia was less well off in 2003 than it had been earlier and admitted that it had not expected stagnation in Africa. It did not foresee that financial crises would be more frequent and did not expect recovery in Latin America to be so slow.

Above all, some of the most successful countries had not followed the principles of the Washington Consensus. Chile, India, and China, for example, were more open than previously but 'many aspects' of their policies were 'far from compliant with conventional wisdom'. India and China protected trade and state enterprises played a large part in their economies. The Chinese Government has suppressed wages. India had large fiscal deficits with low inflation and low interest rates. Economies, concluded the World Bank, do not operate in 'mechanical ways'.[4]

When the model had been followed, for example, by privatising industry, corruption had sometimes produced perverse results. As the World Bank put it: 'lack of political forces and such institutions as a free press allowed those who were politically well connected to take advantage of privatizations ... while enabling corruption to flourish'. Russia was a prime example. Privatisation also failed to

11

produce the gains expected for growth and investment.[5] Privatisation did not automatically end collusion at public expense. It occurred whether industries were formally in the public or private sectors. Privatisation was meant to sever the link between politics and business but failed to do so.

Nankani said that the central message of the 2005 report was 'that there is no unique universal set of rules'. Policy makers should get away from a formulaic approach and start searching for solutions that would work in particular countries. Most notably, the study highlighted the importance of a better understanding of non-economic factors, including history, culture and politics.[6] But the lesson was not just that good government is superior to corrupt government. Countries with 'remarkably different policy and institutional frameworks' had all sustained growth close to the US rate of two per cent: Bangladesh, Botswana, Chile, China, Egypt, India, Lao PDR, Mauritius, Sri Lanka, Tunisia and Vietnam. Each successful country was 'successful in its own way'.[7]

The World Bank remained committed to some key principles including 'macroeconomic stability, domestic liberalization, and openness' but felt that they had been interpreted narrowly to mean 'minimise fiscal deficits, minimise inflation, minimise tariffs, maximise privatisation, maximise liberalisation of finance'. The deeper truth was that the principles could be implemented in more than one way.[8]

The World Bank also revised its thinking about the free movement of capital. Speaking of the crises in the late 1990s, the 2005 report warned of the risks associated with 'indiscriminate opening of the capital account'.[9] Of the ten economies that received large inflows in the 1990s, seven suffered severe crises leading to large output declines, higher poverty and exchange rate devaluations. Surges of funds into each country pushed up the value of the currency and led to current account deficits and higher short-term borrowing. China and India avoided problems through control of capital movements. India avoided appreciation of its exchange rate by direct control of capital inflows and limiting offshore borrowing. Chile and Malaysia taxed capital inflows.[10]

During the 1980s it was assumed that openness to trade was the key to rising prosperity but countries that reduced tariffs and import controls were sometimes worse off. Liberalisation of trade in Argentina and Chile in the 1980s led to appreciation of the exchange rate and reduced the competitiveness of domestic industries. The World Bank concluded that policies should be selective. Bangladesh and India had opened up different sectors at different speeds. China and Mauritius had established export processing zones. Even though they were contrary to free-trade principles, tariff rebates, subsidised export credits, and transport corridors had all helped China, India, South Korea and Mauritius.[11]

It could not even be assumed that state-owned enterprises were always a bad thing. Spectacular successes had been achieved by some governments. Brazil established an aircraft industry through a state-owned enterprise from 1969 and South Korea got into steel through a state corporation in 1968.

Most troubling of all for the World Bank was its discovery that free trade did not always raise the incomes of the poor, when previously it had been taken for granted that higher incomes for the poor would inevitably follow globalisation.[12]

There is now an extensive literature drawing attention to the lessons provided by developing countries and applying them to all economies, including books by

William Easterly, Alice Amsden, Erik Reinert, Dani Rodrik and Ha-Joon Chang.[13] A new pragmatism is emerging that recognises the importance of competition but which is prepared to accept a more extensive role for government— so long as it avoids the traps of monopoly and full-blooded protectionism.

Ha-Joon Chang of Cambridge University has put forward the most convincing case, so much so that he has been described by Martin Wolf as 'Probably the world's most effective critic of globalization'. Chang argues that a pragmatic industrial policy is feasible without abandoning the insights of market economics. He bases his case primarily on the experience of South Korea and Japan. The Korean economic miracle, he found, 'was the result of a clever and pragmatic mixture of market incentives and state direction.'[14] Was this blend unique to idiosyncratic Korea? Chang contends that every developed country used the same methods during its development stage.[15]

South Korea's government nurtured new industries until they were ready to compete. It used tariffs, subsidies and export support guarantees. The aim of the subsidies was to 'buy time' until companies could export on their own merits.[16] But it went further than subsidies. The South Korean government owned all the banks and some key industries, including steel. For several decades the government controlled all foreign currency and insisted that it was used to import machines and raw materials, not consumer goods. It allowed only approved foreign direct investment. Patents were often ignored and pirating was allowed.[17]

After the Korean War in the 1950s the Korean government encouraged the growth of large firms called chaebols. Government-owned banks supplied capital and the government awarded military contracts. However, Korea differed from other countries that promoted large conglomerates. It penalized poor performance and rewarded success, deliberately emulating elements of market discipline. The government refused to bail out failed chaebols with the result that, of those in the top ten in 1965, only three were still present in 1975, and ten years later in 1985 only seven of the top ten in 1975 remained.[18]

Japan used a similar policy. It offered targeted assistance to key companies like Nissan and Toyota, including government contracts and export subsidies but did not prohibit rivals. Today we have heard of the successful exporting companies, including Nissan, Toyota, Honda, Subaru, and Mazda. But between 1945 and 1960 about 30 companies entered the Japanese domestic car market. Only a few survived more than five years.[19] Because the government did not succeed in preventing the emergence of rivals (despite trying to do so), room was left for the unexpected and the companies we are familiar with today came out on top.

The philosopher Michael Oakeshott distinguished between moral perfection 'as the crow flies' and a practical morality of shared habits that could adapt to the details of each case.[20] A rigid puritanical morality often had unforeseen effects and, in the face of the unavoidable uncertainty characteristic of the human condition, rigid application of any abstract principle will inevitably have unpredictable effects. The imposition of markets 'as the crow flies' is no exception. Every nation should have the self-confidence to choose an approach that works in its own case.

Chapter 3 will look at how this conclusion can be applied in the UK, but first let's consider the second approach to wealth creation mentioned in the introduction, non-interventionism.

15

2

Adam Smith and
Non-interventionism

The last chapter showed how the World Bank and a large number of academics have had second thoughts about the free-market policies of the 1980s and 90s. Some have begun to question capitalism itself. But have recent experiences shown that the thinking associated with Adam Smith and his followers has been wholly discredited? Or has a particular interpretation been found wanting? Certainly the leading critics of the Washington Consensus do not see themselves as opponents of capitalism as such, but rather as champions of a new pragmatism that accepts the value of competition and international trade.

I will argue that the approach that dominated the 1980s and 1990s was a narrow and mistaken interpretation of the case put by Adam Smith and his followers. The mainstream defenders of a liberal free-enterprise system never argued that formulaic non-interventionism (or laissez-faire) was desirable.

A powerful tendency of the 1980s and 90s was to be content with privatising, de-regulating and generally getting the government out of the way. The market was perceived as a natural or spontaneous state of affairs that would emerge if people were released from intrusive intervention. The doctrine still has its adherents. Professor James Woudhuysen of De Montfort University finds the idea that governments determine many of a company's competitive advantages to be ridiculous. It is, he says, 'the unconscious action of market forces' that creates prosperity.[1] A more developed version of the theory can be found in the work of Arthur Seldon of the Institute of Economic Affairs, written during the heyday of non-interventionism. He thought the market and the state were mutually exclusive spheres. Capitalism is 'the system that makes as little use of the political process (which creates socialism) as necessary and as much use of the market as possible'.[2] He rejected limited government in favour of the 'minimal state' in which 'government shall do only what it must'.[3] Capitalism was seen as the natural state of affairs. Capitalism 'rests on the elemental urges and aspirations of the common people everywhere'.[4] This spirit emerges in markets, official and unofficial and in socialist and capitalist economies. Capitalism emerges because 'it is the instrument which people in all societies and stages of economic development instinctively use to escape from want and enrich one another by exchange'.[5] He goes on: 'It is the natural growth that finds a way through, under or over, the pervious concrete of coercion that men with power erect to enforce their pretentious imaginings of political perfection.'[6]

But it is not only that such thinkers neglected the work of earlier writers, they also disregarded the arguments of contemporary writers like Hayek, who was seen as one of the guiding lights of Thatcherism. He had often warned against taking too simple a view and had repeatedly criticised laissez-faire economics. His voice was not the only one to be neglected. Ronald Coase, another Nobel prize-winning economist from the University of Chicago, had also warned that markets relied on substantial regulation. Like Hayek, he had been inspired by an earlier generation of Chicago economists, including Henry Simons and Frank Knight. They too emphasised the importance of legal and cultural institutions in creating the conditions for human freedom to work to the advantage of all. There are good regulations and bad regulations and we can't avoid distinguishing the one from the other by denouncing the whole lot as 'interference'. But let's start with Adam Smith, before moving on to Ronald Coase.

Adam Smith and free trade

As the Introduction showed, Smith believed he was contributing to the science of legislation. He was trying to discover what kind of government would make 'a plentiful subsistence' most likely. He did not assume that the 'natural' state of affairs was the complete absence of government, but was interested in the science of good government. Moreover, his ideas were part of an older movement which began as humanism in the Middle Ages and became modern liberalism from the seventeenth century onwards, although its original champions called themselves Whigs.

Liberalism is not primarily an economic movement. As Acton saw, concern about religion was the original driving force and liberalism was a moral movement first and foremost.[7] The central moral ideal was a reaction to the political and religious absolutism of the late Middle Ages. Liberals emphasised respect for each person—individual life would be better and civilisation would advance more rapidly if every person were allowed to achieve their personal best. This state of affairs would be more likely if the amount of coercion were reduced. As far as possible individuals should be able to lead their lives by mutual agreement with others, not by obedience to commands or blind adherence to the mere convention. It was to be achieved by confining coercion to pre-announced laws, so that individuals could take the legal rules into account as they went about their affairs. Moreover, the subject matter of the law should be confined as far as possible to maintaining rules that prohibited harm to others and that were intended to make a society based on mutual agreement more likely to succeed. Liberals wanted a society based on mutual co-operation rather than royal command or religious decree, so that all could exercise the powers or capacities they had within them. Hence, liberals always emphasised the education of both the young and adults, so that innate abilities were brought to the fore. They also recognised that some people began life with a weak hand. Consequently from the earliest times they wanted the government to provide assistance for the least fortunate, so that they too could add their contribution to the common good. This was the tradition to which Adam Smith belonged. His concern for equality under the law, and to ensure that the law served the common good rather than special interests, and his profound concern to raise standards of education, are the characteristic liberal preoccupations.

Although *The Wealth of Nations* is devoted to discovering how best to create prosperity, Adam Smith did not assume that the most important end of policy was more wealth at any cost to other human aspirations. Consider China today. It has experienced rapid economic growth but its government is an authoritarian dictatorship. It holds significant parts of its territory by force, and shows scant respect for the rights of ordinary citizens. If they get in the way of economic development, they are soon bundled aside. Property rights that protect the poor from the rich are non-existent. The liberalism that emerged in Western countries aimed to create the space for human progress in all facets of life. It happened to give rise to a vast increase in wealth, but if it had not done so, intellectually-consistent liberals would have preferred to be poorer but free. Adam Smith, for example, explicitly considered the relative importance of 'opulence' and found it less important than security.[8]

Let me now turn to the controversial question of free trade. What did Adam Smith have to say about it?

Is free trade always beneficial?

Specialisation tends to lead to lower costs of production and, if people are able to buy at the lowest prices, free exchange should lead to greater prosperity. If true, should anyone who consistently seeks to increase wealth automatically be in favour of the completely free movement of goods, capital and people? Many writers have assumed that Adam Smith reasoned in this way, whereas he was far more pragmatic. He used the example of growing grapes in Scotland to illustrate how tariffs could sometimes be wasteful. He recognised that, using greenhouses and hotbeds, good grapes could be grown in his native land and fine wine made for about 30 times the cost of producing it overseas. People were free to go to that expense if they so wished but, he asked, should foreign wines be banned or subject to huge tariffs to protect a Scottish wine industry?[9] He thought that investing 30 times the cost was a waste and that the money could be put to better use.

Nevertheless, he thought that there were legitimate limitations on trade. He argued that there were two particular occasions when it was 'advantageous to lay some burden upon foreign, for the encouragement of domestic industry'.[10] The first was the defence of the country, which in his day required sailors and shipping above all else. For this reason he favoured the navigation acts, which were calculated to take the shipping trade from the Dutch to weaken their economic strength and consequently their naval power at a time when Holland was the only country that could threaten Great Britain. Even though the navigation acts were the result of 'national animosity',

Smith thought they were as wise 'as if they had all been dictated by the most deliberate wisdom'.[11]

He conceded that there was a disadvantage, namely that, with fewer foreign ships arriving at our ports, there might be fewer foreign buyers and British imports were more likely to be dearer and export prices lower, but defence was 'of much more importance than opulence' and consequently the acts of navigation were 'the wisest of all the commercial regulations of England'.[12]

The high priority he gave to defence also led him to support export bounties on herring exports and whale fishing. The subsidies did not add to national opulence but did increase the number of sailors available for defence. The alternative was to keep a standing navy, but the cost of the subsidy was cheaper and therefore justified.[13]

Similarly, if any particular product were necessary for defence it was prudent not to rely on neighbours for supply.[14] Even if the industry were not economically viable, it might be reasonable to impose taxes to support it in order to avoid shortages in battle. For this reason he favoured subsidies for the export of British sail cloth and gun powder.[15]

The second justification for trade discrimination, after national defence, arose when a domestic tax had been imposed on home produce that put it at a disadvantage against imports. In such cases, an equal tax could be imposed on imports to create what today would be called a level playing field.[16]

Always a pragmatist, in the course of discussion Smith also identified two additional occasions when it might be necessary to interrupt trade. The first arose when another country imposed duties on us. In such a case 'revenge' naturally dictated retaliation, leading to the imposition of like duties on them, said Smith.[17] Retaliation would be likely to encourage the repeal of foreign tariffs and the inevitable extra expense was justified in order to gain trade. However, the action could lead to an increase in prices that would outweigh the losses to those injured by foreign tariffs and politicians must judge in each case whether it was worth the cost or not. He was inclined to err on the side of free trade, but the right course, he thought, was a 'matter of deliberation'.[18]

The second additional situation arose when removing barriers would disrupt the lives of a large number of people.[19] He conceded that there was a danger that some groups would exaggerate the harm they were suffering but felt that losses should not be imposed suddenly.[20] Dislocation could cause severe hardship, even starvation. Change should be slow to give people time to adjust—a warning that advocates of 'big bang' change today could have heeded.[21] In particular, he was thinking of occasions when the bad policy of one country could make a wise policy impossible for Britain. Rules governing the export and import of corn, for example, could cause starvation if changed too rapidly. But he warned that such policies should be followed only in cases of urgent necessity.[22] His principal argument was that ending wage control (the statute of apprenticeship) and the control of movement (the law of settlement) would mean that the 'occasional disbanding' of a class of manufacturing would lead to little lasting hardship. However, competition from foreigners should 'never be introduced suddenly, but slowly, gradually, and after a very long warning'.[23]

Perhaps more surprisingly, he also favoured trade measures whose primary purpose was to increase home output, regardless of security needs. The export of raw wool had long been banned because it was believed that the real money was to be made from the processing and preparation of finished products. England would never have prospered if it had remained a nation of sheep farmers. Adam Smith opposed the ban, but not because he objected to any measures that gave an advantage to home producers. His concern was that the ban betrayed the principle of equal treatment under the law. It harmed sheep farmers for the sole purpose of benefiting wool manufacturers 'contrary to that justice and equality of treatment' owed to all subjects by the government. Instead of a ban he favoured a tax on exports of raw wool, which he felt would hurt the interests of farmers less and still give a 'sufficient advantage' to British manufacturers compared with foreign rivals.[24] A 'considerable tax' on wool export was justified, he thought.[25]

Similarly, he supported the exemption from duties that applied to the import of both sheep's wool and cotton wool, both raw materials of manufacture. The exemptions may have been the result of the private interests of manufacturers but were 'perfectly just and reasonable' because the general public gained.[26]

Smith is well known as a critic of the mercantilism of his time, a doctrine that aimed at encouraging a favourable balance of trade. Smith opposed policies that aimed purely to increase exports and reduce imports but as we have seen he was not against tariffs, internal taxes and subsidies that aimed to increase prosperity. He pointed out that a nation could maintain an excess of imports over exports for many years leading to an increase in overseas debts, 'and yet its real wealth, the exchangeable value of the annual produce of its lands and its labour' may have been increasing. He preferred to focus on a second balance, namely that of the 'annual produce and consumption' which 'necessarily occasions the prosperity or decay of every nation'. Such a balance also existed in a nation with no external trade. The balance of production and consumption could be constantly in favour of a nation, while the balance of trade was against it.

24

To ensure that production exceeded consumption was the key to prosperity, not the balance of external trade. If, as the experience of the American colonies had shown, the exchangeable value of the annual produce exceeded that of national consumption, then the capital of the society would increase.[27] Smith's argument holds true today, but in the UK the unfavourable balance of trade reflects an excess of domestic consumption over production that can not continue. Of course, an aggregate like the current account deficit is the result of adding up the economic activity of the many people and organisations who live in the UK. Some private individuals and organisations have over-borrowed and some have not and each must solve their own problem. It is a concern for all of us, however, because our government has pursued a fiscal policy it could not afford.

Smith and Keynes

The lessons to which Adam Smith drew attention have been treated as if they were universal truths that can be reduced to formulaic policy prescriptions. International trading is a mutually beneficial activity much of the time, but in the short run there are winners and losers. Sometimes the losers are concentrated in particular countries and remain the losers for a long time. This has been the predicament of many African countries in recent years. A country that is struggling to pay its way is entitled to a bit of space to gain sufficient prosperity to become a valued trading partner. For this reason the World Trade Organisation permits less-developed countries to impose more controls on trade. Sometimes, however, already-developed countries have significant groups within them who are not flourishing, a problem that concerned Keynes in the 1930s.

In the previous decade Keynes had been in favour of unfettered free trade but, like Smith, he too was pragmatic. He accepted that generally we are all better off when we specialise and trade with each other. However, he wondered what happened to people who had little or nothing to offer. We assume that people shaken out in the competitive process will move to more productive work elsewhere, but sometimes they simply become unemployed. If car production were lost, would all the workers end up in more productive activity at higher wages? He thought that the protection of car manufacture since World War One had been 'wise and beneficial'. Our national aptitudes were suited to it and the results by 1932 had been a 'triumphant vindication of the protection we gave it'.[28]

He did not want large scale or general protection and nor did he want a strategy of national self-sufficiency, but he did believe that we were well-adapted as a nation to make cars and steel and should not allow short-term fluctuations to bring whole industries down. Many countries were capable of making cars and steel, Britain included. Free traders, he said, had 'greatly overvalued the social advantage of mere market cheapness'.[29] It was permissible for public policy to 'buy time' until companies could be self-supporting.

Setting an example of reciprocity

In the same essay Keynes responded to critics who thought that all protectionism was the result of national selfishness. Sometimes it was, but it need not be, he thought. At the height of the Depression Keynes argued in favour of a small import tariff. Although the resulting prosperity might be in some sense at the expense of others who might be more productive in the short run, in practice he thought that Britain would not be selfish in the use of any wealth she earned. He argued that the British people should use any increased wealth responsibly and believed that, in practice, they would. Any gain to Britain would be only a short-term advantage that would be shared through trade.[30] We would not only buy imports but also invest overseas. Preserving our own prosperity was not, therefore, a zero-sum game. Increased wealth would enable us to trade with others on mutually agreed terms. It was not a 'beggar-my-neighbour' policy. To be in a position to trade with others, people have to be prosperous enough to buy products in the first place. Subsidised prosperity is only a first step in an attempt to make ourselves useful to potential trading partners.

Keynes was presumably comparing Britain with America, whose government behaved counter-productively in the 1930s. Today China is pursuing a similar one-sided strategy of national advantage at the expense of others. Trade should not be a kind of non-violent struggle for national supremacy. Its essence is mutual advantage and no nation should press its advantages too hard. In normal business dealings, bargains are struck, but companies value regular relationships and reliable suppliers and invariably do not take advantage of every bit of bargaining power they have at any one time. So it should be in international relations.

Human balance

There is also a human dimension to free trade, which can be seen more clearly in the context of each national community. In a 1932 talk for the BBC Keynes began by declaring his commitment to free trade. We are all individually or in groups richer if we concentrate on 'those activities for which we are best fitted', become specialists in the production of certain articles, and live by exchange

27

with other specialists.[31] It was 'a waste and a stupidity for us to make one thing inefficiently when we might be better employed making something else'.[32]

But, he added a significant qualification. There are some important ways in which tariffs could be based on a 'broader conception of the national economic life and a truer feeling for the quality of it'. Above all, protectionists had sometimes seen the wisdom of not unduly sacrificing a part of society to the whole:[33]

> The virtues of variety and universality, the opportunity for the use of every gift and every aptitude, the amenities of life, the old established traditions of a countryside—all those things, of which there are many, even in the material life a country, which money cannot buy, need to be considered.[34]

How far should we take the search for low prices?

> If it were true that we should be a little richer, provided that the whole country and all the workers in it were to specialise on half-a-dozen mass-produced products, each individual doing nothing except one minute, unskilled, repetitive act all his life long, should we all cry out for the immediate destruction of the endless variety of trades and crafts which stand in the way of the glorious attainment of this maximum degree of specialised cheapness?[35]

He thought not and that consequently the case for free trade had left something out. We should consider the cost of uprooting people from their homes. We should not, for example, aim for steel to be as cheap as possible: 'I wish to see the blast furnaces of the north-east roar again and ships of British steel sail out of the Clyde. And I am prepared, if necessary, to pay a little for the satisfaction.'[36] The pursuit of agriculture too was 'part of a complete national life'. A country that 'cannot afford art or agriculture, invention or tradition, is a country in which one cannot afford to live'.[37]

The case for moderate protectionism has been made more recently by Ha-Joon Chang of Cambridge University. Traditionally many free-market economists have accepted that 'infant industries' may need some time to develop the strength to face established international rivals. Chang argues that established companies that get into difficulties may also need time to adjust and contends that 'adjustment protectionism' should be accepted by the WTO. Insisting on the rapid opening up of nations to international competition can harm both early development and undermine the adjustment of existing companies. He strongly criticises the richest countries who control the IMF and the World Bank for insisting as a condition of aid that less-developed nations face immediate competition.[38] Critics of Chang's view say that the subsidies or tariffs tend to become permanent, but the evidence is that sometimes they do and sometimes they don't.

How far can a government go in assisting economic development without abandoning liberal ideals? As argued earlier, economic policy should be seen in the context of liberal humanism. A utilitarian strategy based on calculative individualism that measured results in purely material terms would be a mistake. So too would pure non-interventionism. Liberal humanism recognises that to live in a free society is to live under a state committed to civic freedom. It is freedom within the law. It also recognises that culture and tradition may embody the wisdom of the ages, as Burke and Hayek showed. But families and individuals come first. The obvious fact that we are 'social animals' and not 'isolated individuals' does not provide a rationale for the exercise of power by any ruler. The purpose of the state is to defend a free life, and the embedded wisdom of our inherited culture must stand the test of human reasoning. Yes, as Hayek and Popper warned, we must not presume too much, as did the logical positivists who thought that, if there were no obvious reason for one tradition or another, then it was meaningless. And we should avoid the presumption of some modern scientists who are inclined to demand political action based on what 'the science is telling us', without the modesty and openness to doubt that should accompany any genuinely scientific conclusion.

The state is a useful administrative agency for advancing human freedom, but as Oakeshott showed, it has a dual role. To make his point he contrasted two socio-political models: 'civil association' and 'enterprise association'. They were the ends of a continuum on which particular nations can be placed at any one time. A civil association is a nation whose members live under shared laws designed to make possible a free life. Such a nation, however, is simultaneously a common enterprise with someone in charge.[39] Depending on the problems it faces, and especially any external threats, a country may need on occasion to become more of an enterprise than a civil association. This was most obviously so when Britain had to transform itself into a unified enterprise to defeat the Nazis under the leadership of Churchill. But such leadership was only welcome for a time and as soon as the danger passed we reverted to the default position: 'civil association'.

Even when we have permitted our government to assume widespread powers, the aim has been to protect freedom, not to allow the government to take over the tasks that properly belong in civil society. Critics of excessive government power are right to highlight the dangers and we should always expect anyone who wants the government to assume new powers to provide some very good reasons. Above all we should ask whether any proposed extensions of its remit enhance the freedom of the individuals who live here. For example, would more people be able to achieve their personal best? When we contemplate measures to encourage manufacturing these are among the considerations we should bear in mind.

Non-interventionism and the importance of institutions

A few remarks about the importance of institutions should also be made, based on the work of Ronald Coase, winner of the Nobel Prize for Economics in 1991. According to Coase, economists tended to 'paint a picture of an ideal economic system, and then, comparing it with what they observe (or think they observe), they prescribe what is necessary to reach this ideal state without much consideration for how this could be done.' But, he argued, 'Economic policy involves a choice among alternative social institutions, and these are created by the law or are dependent on it.'[40]

He criticised those economists who were inclined to see laws and regulations as attempts to restrain competition or create monopolies. They failed to see 'that they exist in order to reduce transaction costs and therefore to increase the volume of trade'.[41] Transaction costs were in Coase's original terminology, the costs of using the price mechanism. Usually they are put into three categories: the cost of finding information (discovering who to deal with); the cost of bargaining and making a decision; and the expense of policing and enforcing agreements.[42]

Coase was somewhat scathing about the prevailing assumptions among many of his fellow economists. Microeconomics, he said, was 'held together by the assumption that consumers maximise utility (a non-existent entity which plays a part similar, I suspect, to ether in the old physics) and by the assumption that producers have as their aim to maximise profit or net income'. But, focusing on 'choice' as an approach had meant that the subject of study lacked substance. The consumer was perceived as 'not a human being but a consistent set of preferences'.[43] Firms had a cost curve and a demand curve and sought optimum prices and input combinations.

Exchange took place without any specification of its institutional setting: 'We have consumers without humanity, firms without organisation, and even exchange without markets.' On the contrary, said Coase, the rational utility maximiser of economic theory bore no resemblance to real people. There is no reason to suppose that people are engaged in maximising anything. Ironically it would be more plausible to say that they maximised 'unhappiness'.[44]

He thought it more reliable to assume that, as a general rule, people who trade will 'engage in practices which bring about a reduction of transaction costs'. Production and trade could be carried out by means of many individual contracts, but in practice firms tended to emerge to organise what would otherwise be market transactions whenever the cost was lower.[45] Firms avoided using the price mechanism when it was too costly.[46]

Surprisingly, he argued that in economics 'the market has an even more shadowy role than the firm'. Markets are institutions that 'exist to facilitate exchange, that is, they exist in order to reduce the cost of carrying out exchange transactions'. Much economic theory tended to assume that there were no transaction costs, in which case said Coase, there was no need for a market. Economics tends to ignore 'the institutions which facilitate exchange'.[47]

The properties of markets were easier to discern in earlier times when markets and hiring fairs tended to be confined to a physical location. In such cases the rules were enforced by local courts of 'piepowder' with jurisdiction over buyers and sellers. Commodities and stock exchanges too were organised by groups of traders who owned the physical location and enforced the rules. Exchanges continue to be regulated in great detail, with machinery for settling disputes and enforcement of obligations. Dealers had an interest in selling to more people and an exchange could enforce discipline by withholding the ability to trade.

It is not without significance, said Coase, that these exchanges—often used by economists as examples of a perfect market and perfect competition—are 'markets in which transactions are highly regulated'. It suggests that 'for anything approaching perfect competition to exist, an intricate system of rules and regulations would normally be needed'.[48]

Under modern conditions it is obviously not possible to confine all exchanges to physical locations where trade can be denied to unscrupulous individuals, and so a state legal system fills the gap.[49] Now is not the time to explore these arguments further, but their significance for our present concern is that doctrinaire non-interventionism treats all government action as nothing but a restraint, when it may be an essential building block of a free system as well as indispensable for the attainment of greater productivity. To be free entails regulation. Non-interventionism offers no escape from the necessity to judge whether or not specific regulations are destructive of commerce or wise supports for enterprise.

Hayek was also a strong critic of non-interventionism. The government should not use its powers to 'reserve for itself activities which have nothing to do with the enforcement of the general rules of law' but there was no violation of liberty if it engaged in 'all sorts of activities on the same terms as the citizens'.[50] According to Hayek, for writers such as Smith and Mill, freedom of economic activity 'meant freedom under the law, not the absence of government action'. They did not mean that government should 'never concern itself with any economic matters'.[51]

Hayek noted that in *On Liberty* Mill went so far as to say that the case for free trade rested on grounds different from the case for liberty:

the so-called doctrine of Free Trade ... rests on grounds different from, though equally solid with, the principle of individual

33

liberty asserted in this Essay. Restrictions on trade, or on production for purposes of trade, are indeed restraints; and all restraint, *qua* restraint, is an evil: but the restraints in question affect only that part of conduct which society is competent to restrain, and are wrong solely because they do not really produce the results which it is desired to produce by them. As the principle of individual liberty is not involved in the doctrine of Free Trade, so neither is it in most of the questions which arise respecting the limits of that doctrine.[52]

Hayek thought that many government measures were not justified because they did not work but, he said, 'they cannot be rejected out of hand as government intervention but must be examined in each instance from the viewpoint of expediency'.[53] Of course, it was very difficult to prevent the government from using its coercive powers, and so there should be a presumption against taking on additional activities but this did not mean that 'all state enterprise must be excluded from a free system'. What is objectionable, he said, was 'not state enterprise as such but state monopoly'.[54]

The range and variety of government action that was, at least in principle, reconcilable with a free system was considerable, he thought:

> The old formulae of laissez-faire or non-intervention do not provide us with an adequate criterion for distinguishing between what is and what is not admissible in a free system. There is ample scope for experimentation and improvement within that permanent legal framework which makes it possible for a free society to operate most efficiently. We can probably at no point be certain that we have already found the best arrangements or institutions that will make the market economy work as beneficially as it could.[55]

The continuous growth of wealth and technological knowledge which a free system made possible, said Hayek, 'will constantly suggest new ways in which government might render services to its citizens and bring such possibilities within the range of the practicable'. Decisions about the tasks of government should be made in the same way as decisions in a competitive market. We should keep an open mind and aim to discover through trial and error what seems to work best.

National rivalry

Before turning to public policies, one more concern should be debated. One of the realities that no government can escape is that nations often compete with each other to attract major companies to their territory. Despite WTO and other rules, there continues to be considerable scope for subsidising companies to persuade them to locate in one country rather than another. Nissan, for example, recently received British government support for its planned battery production plant. The government grant was necessary to prevent the factory being built in Spain. No government committed to the well being of its people can realistically avoid taking part in such contests.

As David Merlin-Jones has shown, during the Thatcher years great effort was expended to encourage foreign companies to establish factories in Britain. Nissan was attracted to Sunderland in 1984, partly by subsidising the cost of land, which was provided at agricultural prices. By 1989 about 100 Japanese firms were employing 30,000 Britons.[56]

Mrs Thatcher recognised that governments were in an economic contest and acted accordingly, as her remarks to Parliament in 1981 testify: 'We have gained considerable contracts. The Government have operated behind private companies when we have been negotiating contracts overseas. We have achieved a very great measure of success.' Every other country was helping companies so why not the British Government? She said with some pride that 'Foreign Governments stand behind their companies when contracts are negotiated. On occasion, they add aid to those contracts; so do we. We are operating on a similar basis and winning contracts in the teeth of international competition.'[57] As a result of Thatcher's pragmatic interventionism we now have a comparative advantage in car manufacture.

Contrary to the common tendency at the time to condemn 'lame ducks', companies that got into difficulties were often helped, but only to restore them to independence. British Steel, for example, was competing with foreign companies, some that were nationalised and some subsidised. If the Government had acted as if it were in a free market it would have had to let British Steel go under. Instead it restored the firm to fighting fitness and privatised it when it was ready to stand alone. British Steel was given £450 million in state aid in 1980 and Mrs Thatcher made her motives clear: 'We want the British Steel Corporation to be able to compete with any company in the world, on price, on quality, on delivery'. We know, she said 'there is a lot more money to be earned, because other steel companies are managing to have the output with very, very, far fewer people'. Her government, she said, was investing in the long-term ability of British Steel to compete internationally.

British Steel was not alone. When the computer firm ICL got into difficulties in 1980 it too was helped, not in this case with government grants but by giving a government guarantee for any private loans. Even British Leyland— ultimately to fail—received £450 million but this aid was not a crutch to lean on. It was a reward for having revived its fortunes and increased productivity. Thatcher told Parliament in 1981 that the grant was 'not to enable them to carry on as they were but to help them to carry out the necessary radical restructuring, so that they, too, can contribute eventually to the recovery'.

Her policies were interventionist but intended to encourage competition. The Government did not remove itself from the economy, as some free marketeers assume. Three policies stand out. First, government grants, loans and subsidies were used to 'buy time' so that companies could restructure and become fit enough to face international competition. But the default position was free enterprise and when companies were ready to compete, private ownership was restored. Second, foreign manufacturers were recruited, sometimes entirely as a result of government subsidies or pledges. And third, 'golden shares' were used to restrict foreign ownership of strategic industries.[58]

Conclusions

Supporters of a market economy typically have two main reasons for their enthusiasm. The first is that a market economy helps to uphold liberty. By facilitating human relations based on consent rather than compliance and by encouraging pluralism and the dispersal of wealth, it discourages political absolutism. The second reason is that it produces wealth. Those who emphasise its productive qualities usually divide into two main camps.

One might be called formulaic economism. It is the abstract model of economic life aimed at achieving allocative efficiency described earlier by Coase: an ideal view of a market is compared to real life, which usually falls short. The rival approach is the idea of a market as a process of discovery that reveals new possibilities and allows us to adapt to the uncertainty that is an inescapable part of the human condition.

This second approach—the market as a voyage of discovery—is compatible with individual liberty, whereas formulaic economism is not. One of the main problems we face is that some defenders of a market economy think they have to defend formulaic economism and they often do so with the zeal of someone who wants to uphold individual liberty and guard against political absolutism. In truth they are very different ideas. The search for allocative efficiency lends itself to central direction as easily as to non-interventionism. But even when it is combined with blanket hostility to government 'interference' it fails to recognise that guarding against the abuse of political power requires frequent active efforts by the government—not least to prevent economic power being translated into political power. As Hayek repeatedly recognised, maintaining a free society calls for constant improvement in our laws and institutions.

3

What Should the Government Do?

The aim of policy should be to facilitate prosperity where it is desired, tempered as always by other worthwhile ideals. Why focus on manufacturing? There are two main reasons. First, it is very difficult to become prosperous without a significant manufacturing sector. Wealth is the result of adding value and manufacturing is one of the ways of doing so. Moreover, historically manufacturing has allowed the spread of wealth throughout the population, unlike countries whose wealth depends on natural resources like oil or precious metals, where it tends to remain concentrated in a few hands.

Second, manufacturing is important if we are to have a balanced economy. There are two dimensions to balance: the economic balance and the human balance. In a highly uncertain world it is advisable not to be too dependent on one economic activity. Having too many eggs in one basket makes a society vulnerable to sudden changes in other parts of the globe. Our over-reliance on the City for income while deriding manufacturing as a 'sunset industry' is a painfully obvious example. Of equal importance, a good society should provide opportunities for the talents of all its people. There will be many aptitudes best suited to the combination of practical and intellectual skills needed for manufacturing.

In an earlier publication, *Nations Choose Prosperity*, I argued that much of what makes for success by individuals or companies depends on the conditions created by the government. To take but one very obvious example, a company might make a product with the most modern equipment available and deploy only the labour necessary for the most efficient output, and yet find that it cannot compete in overseas markets because of an unfavourable exchange rate that is the result of wasteful government expenditure that has led to increased debt and higher interest rates. Nearly everyone agrees that we should try to create favourable conditions for free enterprise and that taxation, government spending, and regulation are among the policies that must be got right. But there is controversy in two main areas: first, selective assistance for individual companies or economic sectors; and second, the choice between unfettered free trade and legitimate safeguarding of the interests of home producers and consumers. Some writers oppose all selective assistance and some are against any policy that reduces the unconstrained flow of goods and capital. Let's focus initially on the areas that are least controversial.

Comparative advantages the government alone can create

People living in the UK can't compete on the cost of labour alone. We must therefore create other comparative advantages. Many such advantages are created by companies themselves, but the government can also create some. More to the point there are some that it alone can create. The government should ask what it can do to create comparative advantages without unacceptably compromising our commitment to free trade and liberal-democratic government. Some such advantages are mainly political in nature. Martin Wolf, for example, has argued that stable, sophisticated and uncorrupt political institutions need to be in place before financial liberalisation is possible.[1] A stable and largely uncorrupt system is one of our comparative advantages and for us the main challenges are financial and economic. The strategy should be to create those advantages that are subject to the government's influence, including the exchange rate, government debt, inflation, the official interest rate (the cost of capital), taxes, energy costs, communications, transport links, the regulation of workplaces and the availability of highly skilled employees. Of course, a government rarely has total control. The exchange rate, for example, is subject to many other forces, but a government can realistically hope to exert some influence whereas a single company could entertain no such aspiration.

Macroeconomic policy

There is a close and unavoidable connection between monetary policy, fiscal policy and the exchange rate. The primary aim should be sound money, that is to follow a monetary policy that avoids inflation and deflation.[2] Within the necessary constraints of monetary policy, the government should aim to maintain an exchange rate against key currencies that will encourage exports. Policy should try as far as possible to ensure the export prices reflect the skill and ingenuity of producers, not the vagaries of the exchange rate.

A wise government will try to maintain a balanced budget over the economic cycle, keep national debt low and follow a monetary policy that will avoid inflation and deflation by keeping the money supply proportionate to the production of goods and services. A government that maintains a balanced budget over the economic cycle will tend to avoid debt, which will help to keep interest rates low. When interest rates are low investment based on borrowing tends to be cheaper. To keep the exchange rate low, the aim of policy should be to reduce the national debt to as near to zero as possible over a decade or so.

Over the last few years there has been a tendency to assume that the decline of manufacturing was inevitable because of the higher costs of production in Britain, especially labour costs, compared with those of overseas rivals. But high export prices reflected the exchange rate among other things. In addition to the impact of high interest rates intended to combat inflation, the exchange rate was strongly influenced by the availability of oil and natural gas from the 1980s. The first country to experience a loss of manufacturing due to the discovery of natural gas was the Netherlands. When gas production began, the strengthening exchange rate led to a decline of manufacturing, a tendency that came to be called the 'Dutch disease'. Other countries that followed tried to avoid the difficulty. Norway, has significant oil reserves and established a state petroleum fund in 1990 (renamed the pension fund in 2006) to preserve income from oil for future generations and to avoid using it for current spending. We allowed our manufacturing to decline disastrously while the pound was strong and we now need to take measures to compensate for these errors. That is why the government should set an exchange rate target compatible with increased exports. It will always be difficult to achieve in the face of external events, and the higher priority of maintaining sound money will not always work in the same direction, but nevertheless a sustained attempt should be made. Awareness of the power of external forces should not become a rationale for fatalism. There will be long periods when a beneficial influence can be exerted by the government and the opportunity should not be missed.

Corporation tax

The current rate of corporation tax is somewhat higher than in many rival countries and we should aim to give companies based in Britain an advantage—in part to make up for the unhelpfulness of recent macroeconomic policy. We now face several years of debt repayment, which is bound to dampen investment. A fuller discussion can be found in a recent Civitas publication by Richard Baron and Corin Taylor.[3] Here I focus on a few primary concerns.

Headline rate: Since 1984 the headline rate of corporation tax has been reduced substantially. The 1984 Budget announced a cut in the main rate from 52 per cent to 35 per cent. In 2009-10 the higher rate of corporation tax was 28 per cent and the small companies rate 21 per cent. How do we compare with other countries? The annual KPMG survey shows that the average rate for OECD members in 2009 was 26.3 per cent and for EU members, 23.2 per cent. These figures compare with our main rate for large companies of 28 per cent.[4]

R&D Tax Credits: In April 2000 a tax credit for research and development (R&D) was introduced. From that year tax relief for small and medium-sized enterprises (SMEs) was 75 per cent, which means that 175 per cent of expenditure (130 per cent for large companies) can be deducted from profits (because R&D is already deductible as a business expense). There is also a refundable tax credit for SMEs if losses are made.

Should tax credits be maintained? Some argue for abolition combined with a revenue-neutral cut in the basic rate. The R&D tax credit cost the Treasury about £580 million in 2008-09, compared with estimated total revenue from corporation tax of about £42 billion.[5] The amount saved would not go very far.

The strongest argument for R&D credits is that there is a 'public benefit', namely that it is a legitimate function of government to encourage basic research that creates knowledge for the benefit of all. The tax credit is only available to companies that bring about a genuine advance in scientific or technological understanding. As the HMRC website puts it, a company must seek 'to achieve an advance in overall knowledge or capability in a field of science or technology through the resolution of scientific or technological uncertainty—and not simply an advance in its own state of knowledge or capability'. It can be argued that such knowledge is a public good and that it is cheaper for the government to give a relief to a private company than to pay for the research itself.

It also offers an advantage to companies at the cutting edge of knowledge in science and technology, organisations that might otherwise find it difficult to obtain funds. Moreover, if it were abolished UK companies would be at a severe disadvantage compared with rivals. In 1996 12 OECD member countries had R&D tax credits; by 2007 there were 21. Science-based innovation is one of our main potential comparative advantages, not least because we still have some strong science-based universities, and government policy should encourage it through the R&D tax credit.

Capital Allowances: From 1984 capital expenditure was treated less favourably with the intention of making the overall package revenue neutral. Until that year 100 per cent of investment in plant and machinery could be deducted from taxable profits, but it was replaced by a 25 per cent per year deduction on a declining-balance basis.[6] Despite the intentions of the government, in practice investment was discouraged. The tax changes of April 2008 made matters worse for UK manufacturers by reducing cash flow, especially by cutting capital allowances for plant and machinery (from 25 per cent to 20 per cent) and removing the Industrial Buildings Allowance (IBA). The aim was to simplify reliefs and allowances, but scrapping the IBA effectively increased the cost of building new factories. In recognition of the burden on small companies the regime for capital allowances has also been reformed. From 2008-09 the first £50,000 spent on plant and machinery could be deducted from profits. The remainder could be depreciated at 20 per cent on a declining-balance basis. However, despite further refinements the position continues to be unfavourable to manufacturers.

A recent EEF report recommended that businesses should be able to elect to treat capital expenditure as a short-life asset for up to eight years because that was the average life of industrial equipment (other than computers). The new depreciation rate of 20 per cent would apply but if the item was sold or scrapped within eight years the balance should be claimable.[7] In the long term it wanted all capital expenditure to be deducted immediately, as was possible up to 1984.[8] The Government has failed to provide favourable conditions and, as the EEF has pointed out, some 35 per cent of its members are foreign owned and highly mobile. Regardless of conditions, they are far less likely to see the UK as their primary location for research, design and development or marketing either now or in five years time.[9]

Ideally companies would be allowed to deduct all capital expenditure in the year in which it is incurred. Many, however, will prefer to allocate it over a period as a depreciation charge. They should be free to show the amount in their accounts as they believe best and pay tax accordingly.

A concordat

Ireland has pursued a successful tax policy: namely, a main corporation tax rate of 12.5 per cent on trading income, straight-line depreciation of capital expenditure over eight years (25 years for buildings); plus R&D tax credits. Non-

45

trading income, including interest, rental income and profit from land deals, is taxed at 25 per cent.

A policy along these lines would give all our businesses a fighting chance. The headline rate of corporation tax should be cut in stages to a low rate close to that of Ireland (let's say 15 per cent), 100 per cent capital allowances should be permitted and R&D tax reliefs should be continued. Like Ireland the lower rate of tax should be restricted to income from genuine trade in goods and services. It should exclude interest, rental income and profits and fees from pure arbitrage, that is the buying and selling of securities for profit as distinct from investing in businesses that trade in goods and services. Moreover, companies should be permitted to deduct from their taxable profits allocations made to reserves to provide for future losses and bad debts, as they can in Japan and Germany.

Above all, Ireland has had a consistently low rate of corporation tax since the 1980s and it would be highly advantageous if our government agreed a medium-term framework to guarantee rates into the future, perhaps in the form of a concordat for prosperity. Stable expectations are vital for business planning.

Taxation of dividends and capital gains

It is often remarked that investment in post-war Britain has lagged behind other prosperous nations, but given the punitive rates of taxation that prevailed into the 1980s it is hardly surprising. As Niall Ferguson observed in *The Cash Nexus*, 'It is hard to imagine much stronger economic disincentives' than those in force from the 1940s to the 1980s. In 1947 the effective top tax rate on investment income was 147 per cent. In 1967 it was not much less at 136 per cent. From 1974 to 1979 the top marginal rate on investment income was 98 per cent, due to the investment income surcharge, which was not abolished until 1984. (In 1979 the higher rate of tax was 83 per cent to which was added 15 per cent on investment income.)[10]

The taxation of dividends has an important effect on companies. From 1997 the dividend tax credit was no longer payable to shareholders who were already exempt from tax (mainly pension funds). Dividend tax credit is an amount deducted from personal income tax to reflect the corporation tax already paid on company profits. In 2009-10 the tax credit meant that the effective tax rate for basic rate taxpayers was zero per cent and for higher rate taxpayers 22.5 per cent.

Capital gains tax (CGT) was introduced in 1965. In 2008-09 the exempt amount for individuals was £9,600 and the tax rate was 18 per cent on gains above the threshold. CGT taper relief lasted from 1998 to 2008. If a business asset was held for two years 75 per cent relief was allowed, which meant that the effective tax rate for higher rate taxpayers was 10 per cent, and for basic rate taxpayers five per cent.

The current rates of tax on capital gains and dividends should be maintained at internationally competitive levels. Ideally the CGT rate should not be lower than the basic rate of personal income tax to avoid giving an unduly large incentive to define income as a capital gain.

De-regulation

The annual survey by the British Chambers of Commerce provides the most reliable estimate of the cost of regulation to business. The 2009 Burdens Barometer put the cost to business at £76.8bn. Some regulations are useful, but strong candidates for reduction include regulations on working time, money laundering, and employment tribunals. Many create costs that are out of proportion to any benefits. The chief cost of employment tribunals is the disproportionate amount of senior management time that is taken up.

The government should declare a moratorium on any new regulatory burdens. Often the EU is behind such regulations and, while we are members, it is not within our power to cancel them. They could, however, be implemented with considerably less vigour, as they are in many other EU nations. Ideally employment tribunals and the laws related to them should be cancelled. However, there is no consensus for such a move at present and, in the meantime, a low cash limit of about £5,000 should be placed on compensation awards in all employment tribunal cases. The effect will be to reduce the number of frivolous cases brought, without preventing the most serious from being considered. In addition the pernicious no-win-no-fee system of paying lawyers should be abolished.

Another cost that could be scrapped results from the efforts of governments to discourage owners from leaving property empty. They are required to pay business rates, but in some circumstances it can discourage companies who own or lease buildings from moving to more suitable premises. Despite temporary concessions granted by the government, in practice the cost of the rates may deter companies from using the most economically efficient premises, a factor that could be decisive for survival in very competitive conditions.

Energy and transport infrastructure

The role of government in providing roads, rail, airports and seaports, as well as the internet and energy is well understood. Good roads and ports are vital to exporters. The achievements of governments in recent years have varied, but currently British industries that rely heavily on energy are at a severe disadvantage with rivals whose governments provide cheap energy.

Energy policy is driven too much by climate change campaigners and insufficiently by the needs of industry. According to a separate Civitas study by Ruth Lea and Jeremy Nicholson, business could be facing additional costs on electricity bills of up to 70 per cent because of 'green' policies planned by 2020. Even the domestic sector could face additional costs of up to 33 per cent. The impact assessments of the *Renewable Energy Strategy* were released in July 2009 and show that the net costs of the strategy for the period 2010-2030 are expected to range between £52bn and £66bn (in 2008 prices). Such costs will threaten the viability of a number of high-energy using industries.

The Government has adopted an official target to try to keep the British energy market among the top three most competitive markets in the EU and G7. Such a strategy is wise, but it is not compatible with recent 'green' announcements. All climate-change policies that increase energy prices should be subordinate to the wider objective of preventing British prices from rising above those of the three lowest-cost markets in the EU and the G20.

Support for exports

It is common for governments to provide export support. It already provides export credit guarantees and consular services overseas. It would be of great value if it also provided an exchange-rate hedging service. It should cover, not only imports of raw or semi-finished materials for use in industries that will add value, but also exports of goods and services. Commercial banks already provide hedging but it can be expensive for small businesses and is not available for all risks. Given that the government has a highly significant effect on the exchange rate it would be reasonable for it to offer a currency hedging facility for exporters for an affordable charge. The Export Credit Guarantee Department's Fixed Rate Export Finance scheme enables UK exporters to offer medium and long-term loans to their overseas buyers at fixed rates of interest. A hedging scheme would be a natural extension of the existing arrangements.

Education and skills

International studies show that economic growth depends on education, but not just the length of time spent in school. It is possible to distinguish between the impact of the time spent and the impact of high attainment. A recent study compared education and economic growth in 50 countries from 1960 to 2000.[11] Years of schooling and attainment in international tests were separately correlated with economic growth. One extra year of schooling in a country increased the average GDP growth rate over 40 years by 0.37 percentage points. But the quality of schooling mattered still more. If a country's score was half a standard deviation above that of another nation, then growth over 40 years was one percentage point per year higher. Both basic and high-level skills mattered. In the economically most successful nations basic skills were spread widely through the population (up to 97 per cent) but high-level skills were also more common. In Morocco, for example, only 0.1 per cent of people had high-level skills, whereas in Singapore it was 18 per cent and in Korea 22 per cent.

Official figures suggest that educational attainment has improved, but independent studies suggest there has been little change. In some cases there is evidence that children have an inferior understanding compared with their peers 15 years ago. International comparisons also show a deterioration and it is now widely accepted that the apparent gains in school attainment at ages 16 and 18 have been the result of lowering standards. Benchmarks for university admission have been lowered so that more students could attend without actually achieving the standard previously required. It allows the UK to look better in international league tables such as the OECD's *Education at a Glance* but has left employers puzzled by the poor quality of many new recruits. University admission should be on merit only.[12] And despite Government declarations of support for science, technology and engineering, the last decade has seen the closure of some university science departments.

The availability of skilled workers is vital to the success of any firm. Governments play a major part in education and our own government is formally committed to increasing the number of people with work-related skills. For example, a National Skills Academy for Manufacturing was established in 2007. The Government has focused considerable attention on apprenticeships but many employers still say that the system does not provide them with the skilled people they need. The aim of policy should be to restore the strong link between employers and apprenticeships. Employers should appoint apprentices as if candidates were applying for a job. The assumption should be that there is a job at the end of process, so long as the student achieves the required standard.

Public procurement

The Sainsbury report of October 2007 argued that an order from the public sector was better than increasing the availability of venture capital and called for 'innovative procurement' by the public sector.[13] The British Government has recently tried to encourage the use of public procurement for economic development. The Small Business Research Initiative was launched in 2001 to encourage innovative government procurement from small and medium-sized enterprises (SMEs).[14] In 2005 a mandatory target of 2.5 per cent of external R&D had to be placed with SMEs. However, it was lower than the proportion many departments had already achieved.

The *Innovation Nation* white paper of 2008 promised to use public procurement (totalling £150bn) to drive innovation and the Defence Industrial Strategy of 2005 was intended to involve contractors in developing our defences. However, despite recognition of its importance too little has been accomplished. Government agencies should devise buying strategies that help to incubate new producers and to encourage the growth of home producers. The huge resources of the NHS, for example, could be used to encourage science and engineering based production in the UK.

Basic research

Expenditure from public funds on research and development (R&D) has compared unfavourably with the United States for much of the post-war period. In 1953 the US federal government funded 54 per cent of total R&D. By 1960 the figure had reached 65 per cent, only to slip back to 57 per cent in 1970 and 47 per cent in 1980.[15]

In the mid-1960s the UK was second to the US in total spending on R&D, but by the mid-1980s it had fallen to fifth, behind Sweden, Japan, Germany and the US.[16] Government funding was also reduced in the UK. From the 1950s until the 1970s it had increased to a peak of about half the total. Then it fell to 39 per cent by 1986.[17]

OECD figures show that, as a proportion of GDP, expenditure on R&D in the UK fell from 2.05 per cent in

1993 to 1.78 per cent in 2005. This figure was a little above the average for the EU 27 (1.74 per cent) but below that for the OECD (2.25 per cent) and well below our main manufacturing rivals. The figure for the USA was 2.62 per cent, Germany 2.48 per cent and Japan 3.33 per cent.[18] In recent years the importance of funding R&D and creating links with universities has been more fully recognised, but low-spending on R&D by the Government and the private sector continue to be recognised problems. In 2004 the Government published a ten-year investment framework for science and innovation. This Science and Innovation Framework is widely considered to have been useful, but much remains to be done.

SELECTIVE ASSISTANCE

Government grants, loans and guarantees

One of the strongest arguments against industrial policy is that the government can't pick winners, but for an emerging group of economists, such as Dani Rodrik of Harvard University, it is legitimate for the government to provide incentives for new activities that will create diversity and new competitive advantages. Rodrik accepts that there are dangers in government action, but he resists the conclusion that all government action can best be understood as 'rent-seeking' by private interests intent on gaining exclusive advantage. It may or may not be. We should be aware of rent-seeking and guard against it, but avoiding subsidies altogether is an over-reaction. If there are to be subsidies they should, he says, be linked to objective tests of performance that are not easy to manipulate, such as export success.[19] In other words it is feasible for governments to finance economic development without falling into the trap of backing people with good political connections rather than good commercial ideas.

53

A recent example of the ambivalence of writers who insist that governments can't pick winners can be found in a Policy Exchange report of September 2009. It was 'not clear why ministers think they can do better than market investors', said the report, but having extolled the market, the next paragraph refers to 'market failures' in high-level research and early-stage investment that might mean that research was 'too low'.[20]

There is a tendency among some economists to denounce any support for manufacturing as 'sectoral favouritism'. However, the government plays an unavoidably major part in creating favourable conditions for enterprise, and even the most diehard free marketeers accept that nations will be better off when their peoples pursue their comparative advantages. A government's task is to serve the people who live within its borders. In order to do so, it should ask itself what comparative advantages are possessed by its citizens and how it could help. It should uphold policies that at the very least do not weaken such advantages and preferably it should reinforce them, and where possible add more. In doing so it will inevitably benefit some sectors of the economy rather than others. It would be foolish, for example, to impose unnecessary regulatory burdens on the City, when financial services are plainly one of the UK's comparative advantages, but such restraint should not be denounced as 'sectoral favouritism'. So too the preservation of comparative advantages in manufacturing should not be classified as sectoral favouritism.

One of the persistent complaints made by entrepreneurs is that some investors have short-termist attitudes. Criticism of short-termism began to be voiced strongly in the 1990s chiefly because Japan and Germany had enjoyed remarkable success in export markets in part because the owners of their companies were said to have had a long-term commitment to their survival. In the Blair years the Myners Report of 2000 was concerned that institutional investors followed an industry-standard investment pattern that focused overwhelmingly on quoted equities and avoided SMEs.[21] The report argued that short-termism was common and that 'peer group' benchmarks gave an incentive to herd behaviour.[22] In 2007 the Sainsbury report on the Government's science and innovation policy thought the problem remained. There was insufficient venture capital and, therefore, special incentives were required.[23]

Individual investors, including friends and family are an alternative source of capital, but they are limited by the extent of their personal wealth. The Government continues to accept that there is an 'equity gap' for investments that are beyond the financial means of most informal investors, but too small to attract venture capital funding. The price range is between £250,000 and £1 million, but the shortage is also severe for businesses seeking up to £2 million — and, for some businesses, it may extend even higher. The EEF claimed in 2009 that funding for companies of up to 250 employees and under £10m turnover was difficult.[24] This 'equity gap' is a barrier to productivity growth. It can slow down the development of innovative start-up and early-stage businesses and constrain the supply of capital for some established businesses that are seeking to expand.

Three main approaches have been taken by the Government: first, tax breaks have been introduced to encourage more private money to be invested in start-ups and growing firms; second, loan guarantees have been provided; and third public funds have been lent to professional managers who then invest in companies according to commercial principles.

Tax breaks: The Enterprise Investment Scheme (EIS) began in 1994. From April 2008 investors could buy ordinary shares in a company or an EIS fund that invested in several firms. Relief is 20 per cent of the cost of the shares up to £500,000 if the shares are held for three years. No capital gains tax is payable on the sale of shares, but if they are sold at a loss then the amount lost can be claimed back, less any income tax relief paid. 12,900 new companies had been established under the EIS by 2005-06 and £5.4bn invested.[25]

Venture Capital Trusts (VCTs) are companies that invest in unquoted companies. Investors are able to spread the risk across several companies by buying shares in a VCT. The scheme began in 1995 and had raised £3bn by 2005-06. From 2006-07 a 30 per cent income tax relief was payable on the purchase of shares so long as they were held for five years. No capital gains tax was payable. However, one of the strongest complaints by entrepreneurs who are committed to the long-term organic growth of businesses is that many investors, particularly those benefiting from tax breaks that require a three- or five-year commitment, enter discussions with a pre-planned 'exit strategy'. Their anticipated exit invariably depends on maximising the tax benefit rather than judging the optimal moment for the development of the business or its underlying technology.

Loan Guarantees: The Small Firms Loan Guarantee (SFLG), operated in partnership between government and 23 lending institutions, has played an important role in enabling loans to be made to SMEs that were unable to offer collateral. In April 2003, the Government introduced a package of measures to enhance the SFLG, leading to a 40 per cent increase in take-up of the scheme. It has subsequently been renamed the Enterprise Finance Guarantee and offers a guarantee for 75 per cent of the loan for a premium of two per cent of the outstanding balance.

Loans can last up to ten years and are available to companies with a turnover of up to £25m. Amounts can be from £1,000 to £1m.

Government loans to investment companies

In the *Bridging the Finance Gap* consultation, published in April 2003, the Government described the Small Business Investment Company (SBIC) model that had operated in the USA for 45 years and suggested that a variant of this approach could be adopted in the UK. The original idea was for the government to offer loans at a favourable interest rate to privately owned and managed SBIC funds. This loan income would be combined with private funds and invested in UK SMEs. If the SBIC made a profit, it would repay the government loan and interest (usually the UK gilt rate), then repay private investors. Any remaining profits would be split between government and the private investors.

Enterprise Capital Funds (ECFs) were based on American SBICs. The underlying assumptions was that there was an equity gap—a market failure—that had to be met by government, and to avoid civil servants picking winners professional managers were appointed to run funds.[26] The underlying view was, not so much that short-termism was rife, but rather that early investment was too hazardous to expect private investors to bear the risk alone. It was in the public good for a proportion of the risk to be borne by the government so long as private investors would continue to bear some losses and thus be deterred from reckless investments.

The government will commit no more than £25m to a single ECF and no more than twice the private capital, whichever is lower. An ECF can invest up to £2m in a company and may co-invest with other investors so long as the total amount invested does not exceed the £2m figure. Ten such funds have been launched since 2006. In April 2008, responsibility for the management of ECFs was transferred to a new body, Capital for Enterprise Limited (CfEL). The government hoped that returns from successful ECFs would balance out any losses from those that were not successful.

Early Growth Funds were established to provide for smaller loans. The government invests in shares so long as there is at least an equal private-share contribution. The funds will provide a maximum of £100,000 for start-up and growing firms, provided they raise at least an equal amount from 'business angels'—investors who in addition to providing capital commit personal time to management. Professional managers are expected to bring angels and entrepreneurs together.

The credit crunch from 2007 onwards added urgency and the Capital For Enterprise Fund was launched in 2008 for high-growth, high-tech companies. In June 2009 the UK Innovation Investment Fund was announced. It is a 'fund of funds' with £150m and an initial life of ten years. It is to focus on technology-based investments and will not put money into companies but into a small number of technology funds who use their expertise to invest in promising ventures.

In 2009 the EEF proposed a Bank for Industry financed from profits from resale of the nationalised banks.[27] The usual model for an industry bank is the Industrial and Commercial Finance Corporation (ICFC), which was founded by the Bank of England and the major British banks in 1945 to provide long-term investment for small and medium-sized enterprises. During the 1950s and 1960s it became the largest provider of capital for unquoted companies in the United Kingdom. The Growth Capital Review, chaired by Christopher Rowlands, considered the idea of an industry bank along with some alternatives, but when the review was published in November 2009, it did not recommend a single industry bank, although it was one of three options. It leaned towards using existing providers of finance rather than setting up an industry bank that would accumulate capital and then select investments through local offices. The two other options were: a 'thin' central structure to collect and hold capital to be invested through existing venture-capital providers; or a co-investment model with existing providers.[28] As a result, Gordon Brown announced that a further institution, a Growth Capital Fund, was to be established. In February 2010, Lord Mandelson announced that the Government was likely to establish a state development bank modelled on the German KfW, originally set up under the post-war Marshall Plan.

Promoting ownership—a better solution?

In November 2002 the report *Enterprise Britain* had set out the Government's philosophy. Its opening premise was that the business start-up rate was nearly half that of America, and we urgently needed to widen and deepen the enterprise culture. It then proceeded to devise additional government schemes to encourage investment and, as we have seen, to neglect the most obvious cause of Britain's record.

Many new businesses are set up by individuals who mortgage their home and borrow from family and friends. If a higher rate of business start-ups is the aim of public policy, the first task should be to cut taxes so that potential entrepreneurs have the means to fulfil their ambitions out of their own resources. In particular the higher rate of income tax and inheritance tax should be cut. The government should also recognise that entrepreneurs are often motivated by the personal challenge of running their own business. They want to test their personal potential for achievement and consequently do not want to relinquish control to banks or private investors who insist on a controlling equity stake. The recent Rowlands report described the desire to retain control as a 'market failure'.[29] But the 'aversion to equity' expressed by about 35 per cent of SMEs was because they did not wish to cede control to people with no strong attachment to the ideals of their business. A government committed to free enterprise should recognise the desire to take personal responsibility as, not only legitimate, but also desirable. It is certainly not a 'market failure'. In any event, proprietor-owned and family-owned companies play a vital role in most European economies. A wise public policy ought to facilitate a diversity of legal structures for human co-operation, but the punitive taxation from the Second World War until the 1980s reduced the cash available in private hands for investment.

Instead of reinforcing the personal responsibility of entrepreneurs, the Government's approach has been to create a variety of new institutions. The paradoxical result of this hostility to private wealth was to make corporate wealth and 'political wealth' the only acceptable forms that the control of significant resources could take. Thus one of the main achievements of egalitarians who professed to dislike capitalism has been the enhancement of the power of the business corporation. A better solution would be to cut personal taxes and inheritance tax in order to release resources for a great flowering of private and family initiative.

Saving and enterprise banks

A more radical model for reform is provided by the German savings banks. In 2007 German commercial banks only held 29 per cent of total bank assets, co-op banks owned 12 per cent and the market leader was the savings banks with 34 per cent. About half of German GDP is produced by small and medium-sized firms—the Mittelstand—often family owned and run, and savings banks and co-operative banks have played a vital part in sustaining them through the recession. Some three-quarters of German firms are clients of savings banks.

The savings banks go back a long way. During the nineteenth century local councils in Germany founded savings banks to encourage thrift. From 1929 they became independent institutions governed by the banking laws of the federal state in which they were located. They subsequently provided the services typical of all banks, but lending was restricted to individuals and organisations within the boundaries of the relevant local council.

Until 2005 all deposits were guaranteed by the federal state in which savings banks were based but in that year the guarantees were removed at the behest of the EU under pressure from international banks who argued that the guarantee was an unfair advantage they did not have. As we now know, when the going gets tough the private banks also expect the state to rescue them.

Savings banks have supervisory boards and executive boards like many large German companies. Two-thirds of the members of the supervisory boards are nominated by the local council and one-third by employees. This political power has not been abused, perhaps because the savings banks are under a clear legal obligation to function according to sound business principles.[30]

They have a social and an economic mission—sometimes called the dual bottom line. They have an obligation to foster savings in each locality and must open an account for anyone who asks. The law stipulates that profit-maximisation is not their primary role, but they must function on sound commercial lines. They operate under the same rules as other banks, including the prudential regulations. They cannot be bought and sold in secondary markets, but they can be taken over by or merged with other savings banks. As a result they are less vulnerable to the short-term herd behaviour of stock markets. However, some German savings banks had invested some of their reserves in German state banks, which in their turn had foolishly bought sub-prime products.[31]

Their local roots make savings banks more efficient in certain respects than commercial banks. In particular, they have the major advantage of being close to borrowers and able to assess risk more effectively. The lack of knowledge possessed by shareholder-value banks tends to lead to the imposition of additional costs on borrowers. Because the deposits of small savers must be kept safe, loans by savings banks are linked to credit-guarantee insurance, thus permitting investment risks to be taken without endangering customer deposits. To further ensure stability and the security of deposits, they have regional associations that spread the risk and a national association to add further to their strength.

How might the introduction of saving and enterprise banks in Britain work? We could establish one in every locality starting with the major towns. They would be not-for-profit organisations run by professional managers who expect to work for an honest living, not to increase shareholder value at any cost. The managers would be supervised by trustees representing the customers. They would attract deposits by providing good market interest rates for savings and be obliged to offer full current-account banking to any law-abiding individual or organisation that asked. Investment in non-bank financial institutions such as pensions and insurance would not be permitted and nor would proprietary trading in securities. Saving and enterprise banks would be required to invest in productive enterprises only within a defined geographical area and cover the risk by credit guarantee insurance. Their duties would include the encouragement of personal independence through saving for people on low incomes and to stimulate responsible private ownership by the owners of productive enterprises. Customers would not be able to lose their deposits because the government would guarantee them against loss (as governments do for all banks). However, to avoid the whole of any loss falling on the government, the Enterprise Finance Guarantee scheme could apply. In return for a premium of two per cent of the outstanding value of the loan, 75 per cent of any loss would be guaranteed.

Above all, the creation of saving and enterprise banks would encourage small and medium sized enterprises, long recognised to be the source of inventive dynamism. It would overcome the shortage of finance for such ventures, a problem acknowledged since the 1930s and for many years called the 'Macmillan gap' after the 1931 Macmillan report on the financing of business and, as we have seen, today called the 'equity gap'.

Regional Development Agencies

England has nine regional development agencies (RDAs) with command of considerable resources. Some critics say they should be abolished. A possible compromise position would be to abolish the top-heavy administrative apparatus of each RDA and to use the funds to invest in productive enterprises, perhaps through local saving and enterprise banks or a new Industry Bank.

Trade and reciprocity

I will approach this issue by asking the questions that, as we saw in chapter 2, Adam Smith raised in his own day.

Government policies can directly increase exports or reduce imports through measures such as tariffs, taxes, and quantitative controls, or they can advantage or disadvantage companies based in the UK in such a way as to increase or decrease both exports and imports. Based on *The Wealth of Nations*, there are six possible questions we could address to any policy proposals.

Smith's six questions

1. **Strategic importance**. Does an industry have strategic importance, particularly for national defence? (Defence is 'of much more importance than opulence', said Smith.) It is generally accepted that nations have some vital interests that governments should protect. Few question the almost universal practice of ensuring a viable defence industry. The importance of food security is also widely accepted, not least by the USA and the European Union. Other nations, including India and Japan, maintain lists of strategic industries and limit foreign ownership. France has been particularly keen on defending a large number of strategic industries. There is particular suspicion of investment by foreign governments through sovereign wealth funds or sovereign pension funds. This is not the place to draw up a definitive list of strategic industries, but the government should have such a list, with defence and all related industries at the top. Foreign shareholding should be restricted to no more than about 20 per cent. During the Thatcher years, for example, foreign ownership of defence-related firms was limited to 15 per cent, although it was later increased to 29.5 per cent

2. **Trade and Reciprocity**. Should the government seek reciprocity in trade? (When another country imposes duties, depending on the cost, it is sometimes necessary to impose like duties on them, said Smith.) We may not want

to emulate the worst overseas practices but our government should not be quiescent in the face of overseas 'beggar-my-neighbour' policies. World Trade Organisation rules allow for reciprocal action to correct unfair trade practices and we should make greater use of its provisions. Smith's approach was rather different from that of Milton Friedman. He argued that if a foreign government subsidised its producers' exports to America, the US Government should not retaliate against 'dumping'. The lower prices should be taken as a gift from overseas taxpayers. Their lower standard of living, he said, was a kind of 'reverse foreign aid'.[32] If Friedman is right, then all export subsidies could be seen as gifts from the exporting country's taxpayers to foreign buyers, not 'beggar-my-neighbour' policies. And if the subsidies are advantageous to home producers and the wider public, then such policies could be seen as mutually beneficial to both the exporting and importing nations. In the short run, however, enforcement of reciprocity is likely to be the most effective.

3. **Government-imposed costs**. When public policies add to the costs of home producers, should equal costs be added to those of importers to avoid unfairly disadvantaging our own firms? (When 'some tax is imposed at home' it seems reasonable that 'an equal tax' should be imposed on foreign producers, said Smith.[33]) When our producers are threatened by overseas suppliers, we should examine how much of the price difference between a home producer and an overseas rival is the result of costs imposed by the British government. If the difference is the result of state-imposed costs, a compensatory public policy remedy is justified. As we saw earlier in this chapter, government energy policies are endangering some of our major industries and it would be legitimate to ensure that home producers are not disadvantaged.

4. **Sudden change**. How can we protect people from sudden harmful change or permit time for gradual adjustments to changed circumstances? (Humanity meant that 'freedom of trade should be restored only by slow gradations, and with a good deal of reserve and circumspection', said Smith.[34]) At the time of writing the Corus steel plant at Redcar on Teesside had been 'mothballed' because a major order had been cancelled. In such a case protection is justified to preserve the 1,600 jobs and to maintain steel production capability in the UK.

5. **Economising**. Is a proposed trade-related measure cheaper than the alternative? (Smith favoured subsidising herring fishing to increase the number of sailors because to do so was cheaper than maintaining a standing navy.) Are there any modern parallels? The R&D tax credit, for example, encourages private research and development. The subsidy can be defended as cheaper than a directly-funded research programme.

6. **The common good or sectional gain**. Is the proposed policy in the common good or does it solely benefit a self-serving section of society? (Smith favoured a tax on the export of raw wool because it 'might prove advantageous to all the different subjects of the state'.[35]) Under modern conditions a government can act to create 'capacity to compete', but it should stop when its measures entrench monopoly or become merely an excuse to impose higher prices on fellow citizens. Opposition to foreign investment need not necessarily be the result of anti-competitive scheming. Controls may well encourage competition. The free flow of capital is often said to be a good thing on the assumption that investors are seeking the best locations for productive activity. However, there are disadvantages. By 2006 40 per cent of UK voting shares were owned overseas, up from six per cent in the early 1960s. In a downturn

foreign owners are far more likely to close UK plants, even when they are economically viable. Sentiment usually plays some part in business decisions and foreign owners are more likely to favour their homeland over the interests of the British people they employ.

Tata steel, for example, the Indian company that owns Corus, has closed the Redcar steel plant because of 'over-production'. However, according to Christopher Booker in the *Sunday Telegraph*, it is about to build a new plant in the Netherlands (with a subsidy from the EU and the Dutch government) and also to build new plants in India.[36] It is not that labour costs in the UK make steel production non-viable. Costs in the Netherlands are similar. It seems that Tata Steel stands to make huge gains by taking advantage of subsidies available from the EU and the UN. Under the EU's Emissions Trading Scheme, by cutting output at Redcar, Tata Steel will earn carbon credits worth £600m in the next three years. Over the same period, production in India is to increase from 54m tonnes to 124m and, because the new plants can be seen as replacements for old 'inefficient' plants, Tata will be able to claim an additional £600m from the UN's Clean Development Mechanism. The closure of the Redcar steelworks has, therefore, nothing to do with concentrating steel production in the most efficient locations. A vital industry will be lost because a foreign owner inevitably lacks commitment to the people of this country and prefers to maximise his income from whatever EU or UN incentive scheme is available. In such cases the government has a duty to step in to protect the national interest.

Moreover, the motive of investors is sometimes to weaken competition or strengthen monopoly. For example, a good case can be made for preventing foreign investment when a foreign company plans to take over a domestic rival, close it down, and thereby reduce competition.[37] In such cases anti-monopoly law should take precedence to ensure both domestic and international competition, which is in the interests of all. Proposed foreign takeovers should all be referred to the Competition Commission to ensure that the outcome will not reduce worldwide competition. Until the 2002 Enterprise Act the Secretary of State could intervene to prevent actions detrimental to the interests of consumers. This general 'public interest' test should never have been abolished and should be reinstated.

Conclusions

We should not pursue policies in a spirit of national animosity or with a 'beggar-my-neighbour' attitude. But we should not be ashamed of legitimate patriotism. In a competitive system all measures to increase exports and reduce imports are to some extent at the expense of someone else in the short run. Such consequences cannot be avoided altogether, but they can be approached in a spirit of reciprocity. As Keynes argued, if Britain were to become more prosperous as a result of the import tariff he had proposed, the government should take pains to ensure that any additional income was applied in a spirit of inter-national reciprocity. We should use our new wealth to buy the produce of other nations and invest overseas to add to their prosperity as well as our own, thus justifying more trade, higher incomes and more widely dispersed wealth. A poor country is not able to be of any real help to other nations. A rich country can do a lot. We should not be squeamish about increasing our prosperity in the first place, but take pains to ensure our acquired wealth is used in an internationally public-spirited way. Doctrinaire free trade neglects any such concerns and, as the World Bank has discovered, it may even fail to achieve hoped-for prosperity.

Summary of Policy Recommendations

1. Set an exchange-rate target consistent with a higher-level of manufactured exports, subject to a monetary policy aimed at achieving sound money.

2. Reduce government debt as rapidly as possible to reduce the cost of borrowing so that investment can be increased.

3. Aim to move towards a main corporation tax rate of 15 per cent within a few years. Preserve and extend R&D tax credits. Move towards 100 per cent capital allowances.

4. Cut personal tax and inheritance tax to increase the funds available for private investment with the intention of encouraging a renewal of private and family-owned enterprises.

5. Apply a moratorium on all new business regulations in the legislative pipeline.

6. Aim to abolish employment tribunals and all related laws, and in the meantime, place a cash limit of £5,000 on all employment-related compensation awards.

7. Abolish business rates on empty property.

8. Restrict all climate-related measures to those that are consistent with keeping the UK within the top three most competitively priced energy markets in the EU and the G20.

9. As an extension of the export credits guarantee service, provide an exchange-rate hedging service for raw and semi-finished materials imported for use in manufacturing, and for exports of finished products.

10. Use public procurement more effectively to incubate innovative companies.

11. Increase taxpayer support for basic research when financial constraints permit.

12. Preserve and extend the Enterprise Finance Guarantee scheme.

13. Develop an Industry Bank, modelled on the Industrial and Commercial Finance Corporation.

14. Encourage saving and enterprise banks modelled on German savings banks.

15. Transform regional development agencies into arms of the Industry Bank.

16. Maintain a list of strategic industries, including defence, support them and prevent foreign takeovers.

17. Make vigorous use of WTO reciprocity rules.

18. Encourage the WTO to permit 'adjustment protection' for a time-limited period.

19. Ensure that importers are not placed at an advantage by home taxes and regulations. If necessary equalise the burden.

20. Examine all substantial foreign investments to ensure compatibility with competition law.

21. Place apprenticeships as far as possible under the control of employers, and whenever feasible provide the prospect of a job at the end.

22. Repeal the 2002 Enterprise Act to allow the relevant Secretary of State to intervene to protect the public interest in cases of acquisitions, mergers and other potentially anti-competitive activity.

Notes

Preface

1 Cohen, N., *Standpoint*, January-February 2010, p. 63.

2 Structured investment vehicles were primarily off-balance sheet devices for circumventing international banking regulations (Basel I) and tended to be concentrated in London because of its light-touch regulatory philosophy. Tett, G., *Fools Gold*, Little Brown, 2009, p. 116.

3 Keynes, J.M., 'Liberalism and Labour (1926)' in *Essays in Persuasion*, London: Norton 1963, p. 341.

Introduction

1 BERR, *Globalisation and the UK Economy*, 2008, p. 18.

2 Kant, I., *Political Writings*, Cambridge: Cambridge University Press, 1991, p. 46.

3 Smith, A., *Wealth of Nations*, Indianapolis: Liberty Fund, 1976, p. 428.

4 Posner, R., *A Failure of Capitalism*, London: Harvard University Press, 2009; Bootle, R., *The Trouble With Markets*, London: Nicholas Brealey, 2009; Wolf, M., *Fixing Global Finance*, London: Yale University Press, 2009.

1: We Are All Developing Countries Now

1 World Bank, Economic Growth in the 1990s, 2005, p. xi.

2 World Bank, pp. xi-xii.

3 World Bank, p. xii.

4 World Bank, p. 9.

5 World Bank, pp. 10,20.

6 World Bank, p. xiii.

7 World Bank, pp. 12, 14.

8 World Bank, p. 11.

9 World Bank, p. 15.

10 World Bank, p. 22.

[11] World Bank, p. 12.

[12] World Bank, p. 19.

[13] Easterly, W., *The Elusive Quest For Growth*, London: MIT, 2002; Amsden, A., *The Rise of 'The Rest'*, Oxford: Oxford University Press, 2001; Reinert, E., *How Rich Countries Got Rich ... and Why Poor Countries Stay Poor*, London: Constable, 2007; Rodrik, D., *One Economics Many Recipes*, Princeton: Princeton University Press, 2007; Chang, Ha-Joon, *Bad Samaritans*, London: Random House, 2008.

[14] *Bad Samaritans*, p. 15.

[15] *Bad Samaritans*, p. 15.

[16] *Bad Samaritans*, p. 15.

[17] *Bad Samaritans*, p. 14.

[18] Nelson, R., *National Innovation Systems: A Comparative Analysis*, Oxford: OUP, 1993, p. 363.

[19] *National Innovation Systems*, p. 100.

[20] Oakeshott, M., 'The Tower of Babel' in *Rationalism in Politics and Other Essays*, Indianapolis: Liberty Press, 1991, p. 482.

2: Adam Smith and Non-interventionism

[1] Woudhuysen, J., at Spiked Online: http://www.spiked-online.com/index.php/site/reviewofbooks_article/7646/

[2] Seldon, A., *Capitalism*, Oxford: Blackwell, 1990, p. 10.

[3] *Capitalism*, p. xi.

[4] *Capitalism*, p. x.

[5] *Capitalism*, p. 1.

[6] *Capitalism*, p. 1.

[7] Acton, J., *The History of Freedom and Other Essays*, London: Macmillan, 1907, p. 52.

[8] Smith, A., *Wealth of Nations* (Liberty Classics edition), pp. 464-65.

[9] *Wealth of Nations*, p. 358.

[10] *Wealth of Nations*, p. 463.

[11] *Wealth of Nations*, p. 464.

[12] *Wealth of Nations*, pp. 464-65.

[13] *Wealth of Nations*, p. 518.

[14] *Wealth of Nations*, pp. 522-23.

[15] *Wealth of Nations*, pp. 522-23.

[16] *Wealth of Nations*, p. 463.

[17] *Wealth of Nations*, p. 467.

[18] *Wealth of Nations*, p. 468.

[19] *Wealth of Nations*, p. 469.

[20] *Wealth of Nations*, p. 271.

[21] *Wealth of Nations*, p. 606.

[22] *Wealth of Nations*, p. 539.

[23] *Wealth of Nations*, pp. 470-71.

[24] *Wealth of Nations*, pp. 464-5; p. 654.

[25] *Wealth of Nations*, p. 653.

[26] *Wealth of Nations*, p. 643.

[27] *Wealth of Nations*, p. 497.

[28] Moggridge, D. (ed.), *The Collected Writings of John Maynard Keynes*, London: Cambridge University Press, vol. XXI, p. 208.

[29] *Collected Writings*, p. 206.

[30] *Collected Writings*, p. 57.

[31] *Collected Writings*, p. 204.

[32] *Collected Writings*, p. 205.

[33] *Collected Writings*, pp. 206-7.

[34] *Collected Writings*, p. 207.

[35] *Collected Writings*, p. 207.

[36] *Collected Writings*, p. 209.

[37] *Collected Writings*, p. 210.

[38] Chang, H-J., 'Industrial Policy: Can We Go Beyond an Unproductive Confrontation?' Paper for Annual World Bank Conference on Development Economics, Seoul, South Korea, June 2009.

[39] Oakeshott, M., *On Human Conduct*, Oxford: Clarendon Press, 1975, p. 222.

[40] Coase, R.H., *The Firm, the Market and the Law*, London: University of Chicago Press, 1990, p. 28.

[41] *The Firm, the Market and the Law*, p. 9.

[42] *The Firm, the Market and the Law*, p. 6.

[43] *The Firm, the Market and the Law*, pp. 2-3.

[44] *The Firm, the Market and the Law*, pp. 3-4.

[45] *The Firm, the Market and the Law*, p. 7.

[46] *The Firm, the Market and the Law*, p. 63.

[47] *The Firm, the Market and the Law*, pp. 7,8.

[48] *The Firm, the Market and the Law*, p. 9.

[49] *The Firm, the Market and the Law*, p. 10.

[50] Hayek, F.A., *Constitution of Liberty*, 1960, p. 223.

[51] *Constitution of Liberty*, p. 220.

[52] Mill, J.S, *On Liberty*, Everyman Edition, pp. 150-51.

[53] *Constitution of Liberty*, p. 221.

[54] *Constitution of Liberty*, p. 224

[55] *Constitution of Liberty*, p. 231.

[56] Merlin-Jones, D., '"Time for turning?" Why the Conservatives need to rethink their industrial policy', *Civitas Review*, January 2010. Online here: http://www.civitas.org.uk/pdf/CivitasReviewJanuary2010.pdf

[57] Weekly *Hansard* HC [10/881-87], 28 October 1981.

[58] TV Interview for London Weekend Television Weekend World, 6 January 1980. Thatcher Archive: LWT transcript.

3: What Should the Government Do?

[1] Wolf, M., *Fixing Global Finance*, London: Yale University Press, 2009, p. 24.

[2] Congdon, T., *Central Banking in a Free Society*, London: IEA, 2009.

[3] Baron, R. and Taylor, C., 'Corporation Tax: Beating the Competition', Online Report, London: Civitas, 2010.

[4] KPMG, *Corporate and Indirect Tax Rate Survey 2009*.

[5] HM Treasury, *Tax Ready Reckoner and Tax Reliefs*, November 2008, p. 14.

[6] Declining balance depreciation works like this. If capital expenditure of £1,000 is incurred and the depreciation rate is 25 per cent then £250 is deducted in the first year, leaving a balance of £750. In the second year 25 per cent of £750 is deducted and so on until nothing is left. It is contrasted with straight line depreciation. If £1,000 is spent and the rate is 25 per cent then £250 is deducted for each of four years.

[7] EEF, *A Manufacturing Future – competitiveness and taxation in the UK*, March 2009, p. 14.

[8] *A Manufacturing Future*, p. 15.

[9] *A Manufacturing Future*, p. 7.

[10] Clark, T. and Dilnot, A., 'Long-Term Trends in British Taxation and Spending', IFS, BN 25, 2002, pp. 7-8; Ferguson, N., *The Cash Nexus*, London: Penguin, 2002, pp. 75-76.

[11] Hanushek, E. *et al.*, 'Education and Economic Growth', *Education Next*, Spring 2008, pp. 62-70.

[12] Rodrik, D., *One Economics Many Recipes*, Princeton: Princeton University Press, 2007, p. 629.

[13] Sainsbury, Lord, *The Race to the Top*, HM Treasury, October 2007, p. 79.

[14] The EU uses slightly different terminology: micro, small and medium-sized enterprises:

http://ec.europa.eu/enterprise/enterprise_policy/sme_definition/sme_user_guide.pdf

[15] Nelson, R. (ed.), *National Innovation Systems: A Comparative Analysis*, Oxford: OUP, 1993, Table 2.3, p. 41.

[16] *National Innovation Systems*, Table 5.9.

[17] Walker, W., in Nelson (ed.), *National Innovation Systems*, Chapter 5.

[18] OECD *Factbook*, 2008, p. 157.

[19] Rodrik, *One Economics Many Recipes*, p. 106.

[20] Policy Exchange, 'Innovation and Industry: the Role of Government', Research Note, 2009, pp. 3-4.

[21] Myners, Lord, 'Institutional Investment in the UK: A Review', 2000, HM Treasury, p. 4.

[22] 'Institutional Investment in the UK: A Review', p. 2, p. 9.

[23] 'The Race to the Top', p. 79.

[24] EEF, *A Manufacturing Future*, 2009, p. 23.

[25] Sainsbury, *The Race to the Top*, p. 89.

[26] HM Treasury, *Bridging the Finance Gap*, 2003, p. 37.

[27] *A Manufacturing Future*, 2009.

[28] http://www.berr.gov.uk/files/file53698.pdf

[29] Rowlands, C., *The Provision of Growth Capital to UK Small and Medium Sized Enterprises*, November 2009, BIS, p. 14.

[30] 'German Savings Banks' in Ayadi, R. *et al.*, *Investigating diversity in the banking sector in Europe: the performance and role of savings banks*, Brussels, CEPS, 2009.

[31] http://www.spiegel.de/international/business/0,1518,536635-2,00.html

[32] Friedman, M., *Free To Choose*, London: Secker and Warburg, 1980, p. 45.

[33] Smith, A., *Wealth of Nations* (Liberty Classics edition), p. 465.

[34] *Wealth of Nations*, p. 469.

[35] *Wealth of Nations*, p. 654.

[36] *Sunday Telegraph*, 12 December 2009.

[37] Porter, M.E., *The Competitive Advantage of Nations*, London: Palgrave, 1998, p. 671.